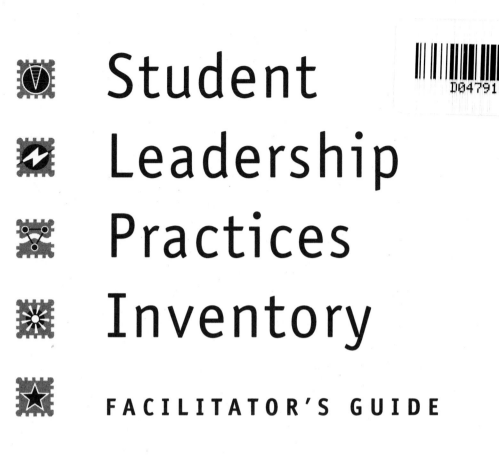

Student Leadership Practices Inventory

FACILITATOR'S GUIDE

James M. Kouzes
Barry Z. Posner, Ph.D.

Jossey-Bass Publishers • San Francisco

ISBN: 0-7879-4424-6

Printed in the United States of America.

Jossey-Bass books and products are available through most bookstores. To contact Jossey-Bass directly, call (888) 378-2537, fax to (800) 605-2665, or visit our website at www.josseybass.com.

Substantial discounts on bulk quantities of Jossey-Bass books are available to corporations, professional associations, and other organizations. For details and discount information, contact the special sales department at Jossey-Bass.

Printing   10   9   8   7   6   5   4   3   2

 This book is printed on acid-free, recycled stock that meets or exceeds the minimum GPO and EPA requirements for recycled paper.

CONTENTS

1   Introduction

Leadership is everyone's business. Our research has shown that leadership is an observable, learnable set of practices. It is not something mystical and ethereal that cannot be understood by ordinary people. Given the opportunity for feedback and practice, we believe that those with the desire and persistence to lead can substantially improve their abilities to do so.

Many young people taking a leadership course for the first time already have more leadership experience than they realize. For example, they may have trained and supervised peers in an employment setting or volunteer activity, started a club, or captained a sports team. A leadership development survey is not only a means of learning leadership skills, but also a way of discovering or examining the leadership experiences students may have had already.

The purpose of this manual is to assist you (the facilitator) in designing and conducting a leadership program based on the *Student Leadership Practices Inventory (Student LPI)*. Using this manual in conjunction with the *Student LPI*, you will be able to accomplish the following:

- Present a valid, understandable, and practical model of leadership for students
- Provide reliable and useful feedback to students on their current use of a specific set of leadership behaviors
- Conduct a workshop (from one hour to a half-day or full day) on leadership
- Integrate the *Student LPI* into other leadership development programs

In addition to its use in leadership development programs, the original *Leadership Practices Inventory* has also been used for leader selection, performance feedback, and leadership research. Therefore, we have designed this manual to be helpful to the individual interested in these alternative uses of the LPI.

The original LPI and the *Student LPI* were created as part of an extensive and continuing research project into the everyday actions and behaviors of exemplary leaders—at all levels, across a variety of organizational settings. Our book, *The Leadership Challenge: How to Keep Getting Extraordinary Things Done in Organizations*,[1] provides a comprehensive explanation of the empirical and conceptual basis for the practices and behaviors that are the foundation of these instruments. It also offers numerous suggestions for improving skills in these practices and behaviors. Consequently, we strongly recommend that all facilitators read this book prior to conducting a workshop or program in which the *Student LPI* will be used. Students also benefit from reading the book, often as a follow-up to their workshop or classroom participation.

We wish you every success in your efforts to liberate the leader within each student.

James M. Kouzes
San Jose, California
May 1998

Barry Z. Posner, Ph.D.
Santa Clara, California
May 1998

---

1. To purchase this book or for further information, contact Jossey-Bass Publishers, 350 Sansome Street, San Francisco, CA 94104. Phone: (800) 274-4434.

2 Origin of the Student Version of the *Leadership Practices Inventory*

Most of the leadership development programs designed for college students are based on studies and models that were developed with managers in business and public-sector organizations.[2] Serious questions can be raised about whether such models and their concomitant instruments are applicable to college students and collegiate environments, which differ considerably from the environments in which managers operate. Based on her review of the literature, Brodsky (1988) concluded that "valid instruments designed specifically for college students to measure their leadership development did not exist." The *student* version of the LPI was developed to fill this gap.[3]

The *Student LPI* has two forms: Self and Observer. Each form consists of thirty statements—six statements to measure each of the five leadership practices. The forms differ only in the individuals who complete them. The Self form is completed by the student leader himself or herself, and the Observer form is completed by a person who has directly observed the leadership behaviors of that student leader. During the workshop or course, students compare the two sets of responses to discover their strengths or areas for improvement as leaders. Within the course or workshop, facilitators can take students through a series of exercises to help them better understand and develop the five practices of exemplary leadership.

Instrument Development

In developing the original LPI, we collected case studies from over 2,500 managers about their personal-best experiences as leaders. Content analyses of these case studies suggested a pattern of behaviors used by people when they

---

2. F. H. Freeman, K. B. Knott, and M. K. Schwartz, *Leadership Education 1994–1995: A Sourcebook*. Greensboro, NC: Center for Creative Leadership, 1994.

3. The conceptual origin of the original *Leadership Practices Inventory* is best described in *The Leadership Challenge*, and its empirical development and psychometric properties are explained in several *Educational and Psychological Measurement* articles.

were most effective as leaders. These behaviors result in the five key leadership practices of Challenging the Process, Inspiring a Shared Vision, Enabling Others to Act, Modeling the Way, and Encouraging the Heart. Subsequently we used the same case-study approach to investigate whether the leadership behaviors of students were comparable with those of managers.[4]

The initial student group consisted of outstanding student leaders, as demonstrated by their nomination for Leadership America, a nationally prominent leadership development experience for college students. Staff and faculty members nominated these students on the basis of a past record of leadership, academic ability, and future leadership potential. Four students were randomly selected by year in school (junior or senior) and gender (male or female) to participate in this stage of the research project.

Each student was invited to participate in the study and agreed to do so. The purpose of the study and the process to be used were explained in a preliminary interview. The students were asked to think about their personal-best experiences as leaders and to make notes about the behaviors they believed were most critical to the success of their endeavors.

One week later, in a structured-interview format, each student responded to specific questions based on the personal-best leadership survey. These interviews served to clarify any language, behaviors, or concepts that might be unclear to students or that did not readily translate from the business world to the world of the college student. The interviews lasted between thirty and ninety minutes; each was tape-recorded with the respondent's consent.

The student interviews were content-analyzed for themes (sentences or phrases) about leadership actions and behaviors. These themes were coded and tabulated into the five leadership categories that we had originally proposed based on experience with private-sector and public-sector managers. There were 264 total responses that were coded for congruence.

The behaviors connected with the leadership practice of Enabling Others to Act were the most frequently mentioned (30 percent). The leadership behaviors mentioned next most frequently were those associated with Modeling the Way (21 percent) and Inspiring a Shared Vision (20 percent). About one-third of the leadership behaviors were coded with the leadership practice of Encouraging the Heart (15 percent) and Challenging the Process (15 percent). These findings indicate that college student leaders do engage in the leadership practices we discovered earlier and that this conceptual framework is relevant to the college student's leadership experience.

Each statement on the LPI was assessed in terms of its congruence with the themes derived from students' case studies of their personal-best leadership experiences. The purpose of this coding was to determine which LPI

---

4. More complete information about this initial research project is available in B. Brodsky, "Development of a Modified Version of the *Leadership Practices Inventory* for Use with College Students," unpublished master's thesis, San Jose State University, 1988. See also B. Z. Posner and B. Brodsky, "A Leadership Development Instrument for College Students," *Journal of College Student Development*, 1992, 33(4):231–237.

statements accurately reflected the behavior of *student* leaders, thus facilitating the process of identifying terminology and concepts appropriate for use with a college-student population. Using this data, we modified twenty-three of the thirty LPI items for use in the pilot version of the *Student LPI*.

The majority of changes, however, consisted of very slight alterations in wording to obtain more appropriate terminology, language, or concept (for example, changing "at work" to "in our group or organization"). Six statements received major changes in language or concept. For instance, "I am contagiously excited and enthusiastic" was changed to "I influence others with my excitement and enthusiasm." Seven statements remained unchanged. Final minor revisions in wording were made based on subsequent discussion with the dean of students and two undergraduate students familiar with the leadership framework.

Pilot-Testing the *Student LPI*

The pilot version of the *Student LPI,* modified to reflect the language and context of student and college experiences, consisted of thirty descriptive statements paralleling those found in the original LPI. Various analyses have shown the LPI to have sound psychometric properties.[5] The factor structure is quite consistent with the conceptual framework, test-retest and internal reliabilities are high, and predictive validity findings are quite reasonable.

Each of the five leadership practices was assessed with six statements on the LPI, each measured with a five-point Likert scale (where "1" meant "rarely" and "5" meant "very frequently"). The statements focused on leadership *behaviors* and on the frequency with which the person engaged in those particular behaviors.

The student senate was asked to serve as the test site for studying the pilot version of the *Student LPI*. This group represented the elected student governing body, with members from all four classes. At the end of one of their weekly meetings, the members of the student senate were asked to participate in the pilot study. Nineteen student leaders agreed to participate (79 percent response rate) on a voluntary and confidential basis. This sample included seven men and twelve women, about equally divided between the four college class years.

After the students completed the pilot version, they participated in an item-by-item discussion to determine whether any test statements were ambiguous, confusing, or not applicable to their experience as student leaders. This discussion was tape-recorded. Of the thirty test items, twenty-five (83 percent) were unanimously determined to be clear and understandable and to consist of terminology and concepts that were within students' and student leaders'

5. B. Z. Posner and J. M. Kouzes, "Psychometric Properties of the Leadership Practices Inventory—Updated," *Educational and Psychological Measurement*, 1993, 53(1):191–199.

experience. Ways to improve the somewhat problematic remaining items were also discussed.

Using the recommendations from the pilot-test respondents, we rewrote the potentially problematic statements. Five student leaders (three men and two women) who had not been involved with any of the earlier *Student LPI* efforts were invited to participate in a focus-group discussion of the revised *Student LPI*. These student leaders were selected from a variety of campus organizations (student government, public service, clubs, and so on). After individually completing the *Student LPI,* they discussed every statement, searching for agreement about meaning and the statement's potential ability to differentiate, in their experience, between effective and ineffective student leaders. We made minor editorial changes based on this discussion. Subsequently we reviewed the changes with the five student leaders, who approved the instrument without modification.

Empirical Studies

There are a growing number of empirical studies using the *Student LPI*. For example, the presidents of a number of fraternity chapters across the United States completed the Student LPI-Self and had the members of their executive committees complete the Student LPI-Observer. The members of the executive committees also assessed the effectiveness of their chapter presidents along several dimensions: building team spirit, representing the chapter to administrators and alumni, meeting chapter objectives, facilitating volunteers, and so on. The most effective chapter presidents engaged in each of the five leadership practices significantly more frequently than did their less effective counterparts. Multiple-regression analyses showed that leadership practices accounted for 65 percent of the variance in assessments of chapter presidents' effectiveness.[6]

A study of sorority chapter presidents from across the United States paralleled the previous study both in design and in findings. The most effective chapter presidents engaged in each of the five leadership practices significantly more frequently than did their less effective counterparts, with the five key leadership practices accounting for 80 percent of the variance in assessments of chapter presidents' effectiveness in multiple-regression analyses.[7]

It was revealed that "the practices of effective student leaders do not vary according to the leaders' gender." Effective chapter presidents, whether male or female, engaged in the five leadership practices significantly more than did the less effective student leaders. This was true both from the leaders' own perspective (Student LPI-Self) and from the perspective of people in their organizations (Student LPI-Observer).[8]

6. B. Z. Posner and B. Brodsky, "A Leadership Development Instrument for College Students," *Journal of College Student Development,* 1992, *33*(4):231–237.
7. B. Z. Posner and B. Brodsky, "Leadership Practices of Effective Student Leaders: Gender Makes No Difference," *NASPA Journal,* 1994, *31*(2):113–120.
8. Posner and Brodsky, 1994.

A study of fraternity pledges revealed that using a systematic model of leadership development enhanced the effectiveness of the pledge education program and significantly increased leadership practice scores (Student LPI-Self).[9] Leadership development as a component of new member development was postulated as a way to better align fraternities with the academic community. The benefits of applying leadership development programming to all students, not to just student leaders, were also articulated as an important opportunity for students to develop their full potential.

In another study, resident assistants (RAs) from seven diverse collegiate environments were the focus leader population.[10] In addition to completing the Student LPI-Self, the RAs distributed Student LPI-Observers to residents in their housing facility. Effectiveness data from the RAs, the students living in their residential units, and the resident director of each campus showed a remarkably consistent pattern: Those who engaged in the five leadership practices most frequently, as compared to those who engaged in them less often, viewed themselves as more effective and were also viewed as more effective by their supervisors and by their constituents. No significant interaction effects between gender and performance were found. The expectations that RAs and their residents have about leadership were the focus of another study using the *Student LPI*. Significant correlations were reported for all five leadership practices in both groups.[11]

The impact of leadership behaviors was also investigated for students serving as orientation advisers.[12] In this study, new incoming college students completed both the LPI-Observer and an evaluation of their orientation adviser's effectiveness. Although the incoming students and their advisers were together for just a few days and arbitrarily assigned to each other, the effectiveness of orientation advisers, consistent with previous studies, was directly related to how frequently they engaged in the five key leadership practices. Self-reports by the orientation advisers (Student LPI-Self) also showed a strong positive relationship between perceptions of effectiveness and the frequency with which they reported engaging in these leadership practices.

Other studies with college students have shown that leadership practices are generally not affected by various characteristics of the group or setting that students are involved in.[13] For instance, students who are being compensated for being leaders do not systematically engage in a different pattern of leadership practices than those who are uncompensated for their leadership responsibilities. Similarly, student leaders working with peers in nonhierarchical

9. C. T. Matsos, "Student Leadership Development as a Supplement to College Fraternity Pledge Programs," unpublished doctoral dissertation, University of Alabama, March 1997.

10. B. Z. Posner and B. Brodsky. "The Leadership Practices of Effective RAs," *Journal of College Student Development*, 1993, 34(4):300–304.

11. M. J. Levy, "Followers' Perceptions of Leaders: Prototypes and Perceptions of Resident Assistants," unpublished master's thesis, University of Maryland, June 1995.

12. B. Z. Posner and J. R. Rosenberger, "Effective Orientation Advisors Are Leaders Too," *NASPA Journal*, 1997, 35(1):46–56.

13. B. Z. Posner and J. R. Rosenberger, "The Impact of Situational Factors on Students' Leadership Behaviors," working paper, Leavey School of Business, Santa Clara University, 1998.

relationships do not engage in these leadership practices more or less significantly than students who are elected by their peers to official positions of leadership or students who hold a hierarchical position in a student organization (such as the office of president).

In addition, it was revealed that students did not vary their leadership practices when involved in a one-time leadership project versus a project or program lasting for an entire academic year. However, students who returned for a second year in a leadership position did engage in each of the five leadership practices significantly more often than those who were just starting in the same position.[14]

While the previous discussion has generally focused on validity, as a psychometric instrument the *Student LPI* has generally shown strong reliability. Analyses from the data of Posner and his colleagues ($N = 1,255$) have demonstrated internal reliability scores of .66 for Challenging, .79 for Inspiring, .70 for Enabling, .68 for Modeling, and .80 for Encouraging. Other published studies have reported internal reliabilities for the five leadership practices ranging between .63 (Challenging and Enabling) and .83 (Inspiring),[15] and ranging as high as between .83 and .92.[16]

---

14. Posner and Rosenberger, 1998. A similar finding on the impact of experience was reported in Levy, 1995.
15. N. L. Snyder, "Empowering Leadership and Achieving Style: A Study of Gender Differences Between Fraternity and Sorority Presidents," unpublished master's thesis, University of Maryland, June 1992.
16. Levy, 1995.

3 The Leadership Practices

In this section we summarize the five leadership practices and associated behaviors that form the foundation of the *Student LPI*. (More in-depth descriptions of each leadership practice can be found in *The Leadership Challenge*.) At the end of each summary are two behavioral commitments that leaders make to put the practice into use (see also the "Ten Commitments of Leadership" in Appendix A). Students and young adults may find they have already demonstrated these practices and commitments in many of their activities—for instance, on sports teams, in school or on campus, in church groups, or in clubs and other organizations. The *Leadership Practices Inventory* will enable many users to consider the leadership skills they already possess as well as to explore the skills they want to develop.

Challenging the Process

Challenge is the opportunity for greatness. Maintaining the status quo breeds mediocrity. Leaders seek and accept challenging opportunities to test their abilities and look for innovative ways to improve the organization. People do their best when there is a chance to change the way things are. Leaders motivate others to exceed their limits.

Most innovations, however, do not spring directly from the leader. Leaders realize that good ideas come through the ears—not the mouth—and listen to the counsel of the people who use their services and products and the people who do the work.

Leadership is closely associated with change and innovation; the quest for change is an adventure and the training ground for leaders. For leaders to get the best from themselves and others, they must find the task enjoyable and intrinsically rewarding. Leaders are experimenters. They find ways to get outside the imaginary boundaries of organizational convention. They take risks—and focus on mistakes as learning opportunities.

The commitments of leaders to *Challenging the Process* involve

- Searching for opportunities
- Experimenting and taking risks

As an example of Challenging the Process, one student related how innovative thinking helped him win a student class election: "I challenged the process in more than one way. First, I wanted people to understand that elections are not necessarily popularity contests, so I campaigned on the issues and did not promise things that could not possibly be done. Second, I challenged the incumbent positions. They thought they would win easily because they were incumbents, but I showed them that no one has an inherent right to a position."

Challenging the Process for a student serving as treasurer of her sorority meant examining and abandoning some of her leadership beliefs. "I used to believe, 'If you want to do something right, do it yourself.' I found out the hard way that this is impossible to do. . . . One day I was ready to just give up the position because I could no longer handle all of the work. My adviser noticed that I was overwhelmed, and she turned to me and said three magic words: 'Use your committee.' The best piece of advice I would pass along about being an effective leader is that it is okay to experiment with letting others do the work."

Inspiring a Shared Vision

There is no freeway to the future; often there are not even paved roads, only uncertain terrain and wilderness. So pioneering leaders rely on a compass and a dream. They look to the future with a sense of what is uniquely possible and passionately believe that people working together can make a difference. Visions are the leader's magnetic north; they give direction and purpose to the organization.

Visions seen only by the leader are insufficient to create organized movement. Leaders must enlist others in a common vision by appealing to their values, interests, hopes, and dreams, so that others clearly understand and accept the vision as their own.

Leaders breathe life into their visions with strong appeals and quiet persuasion, generating enthusiasm and excitement for the common vision. They envision a future full of possibilities.

The commitments of leaders to *Inspiring a Shared Vision* involve

- Envisioning an uplifting future
- Enlisting others in a common vision

Describing his experience as president of his high school class, one student wrote, "It was our vision to get the class united and to be able to win the spirit trophy. . . . I told my officers that we could do anything we set our minds on. Believe in yourself and believe in your ability to accomplish things."

Enabling Others to Act

Leaders know that they cannot do it alone. It takes partners to get extraordinary things in an organization. Leaders create an atmosphere of mutual trust and respect. They build teams that feel like a family and make people feel like owners, not like hired hands.

Getting people to work together begins with creating cooperative goals and sustaining trusting relationships. Leaders understand how being trustworthy is the reciprocal of trusting others. They make sure that when they win, everyone wins.

Empowering others is essentially the process of turning followers into leaders themselves. Leaders realize how power is not a fixed-sum quantity but an expandable resource. The process of strengthening others is facilitated when people work on tasks that are critical to the organization's success, when they exercise discretion and autonomy in their efforts, when their accomplishments are visible and recognized by others, and when they are well connected to other people of influence and support.

The commitments leaders make to *Enabling Others to Act* involve

- Fostering collaboration
- Strengthening people

It is not necessary to be in a traditional leadership position to put these principles into practice. Here is an example from a student who led his team as a team member, not from a traditional position of power: "I helped my team members feel strong and capable by encouraging everyone to practice with the same amount of intensity that they played games with. Our practices improved throughout the year and by the end of the year had reached the point I was striving for: complete involvement among all players, helping each other to perform at our very best during practice times."

Modeling the Way

Leaders have a philosophy—a set of high standards by which the organization is measured, a set of values about how others in the organization should be treated, and a set of principles that make the organization unique and distinctive. Leaders stand up for their beliefs and show by their own example how others ought to behave. Leaders build their credibility by maintaining consistency between their words and deeds.

Being a role model requires clarity about personal values. Focusing other people's energies and commitments requires developing an alignment between the values of the leader and others in the organization.

Leaders get us started by convincing us that the impossible is possible and by taking the first step themselves. Breaking problems into manageable pieces keeps people's capacities from being overwhelmed. Planning small victories moves us off dead center. Small wins breed success and set the stage for building commitment to the new path.

The commitments of leaders to *Modeling the Way* involve

- Setting the example
- Achieving small wins

Working in a business environment taught one student the importance of Modeling the Way. She writes, "I proved I was serious because I was the first one on the job and the last one to leave. I came prepared to work and make the tools available to my crew. I worked alongside them and in no way portrayed an attitude of superiority. Instead, we were in this together."

Encouraging the Heart

Getting extraordinary things done in organizations is hard work. The climb to the summit is arduous and steep. Leaders encourage others to continue the quest. They give heart by visibly recognizing people's contributions to the common vision. They express pride in the accomplishments of their teams. They make people feel like heroes by telling the rest of the organization about what individuals and the team have accomplished.

Leaders have high expectations both of themselves and of their constituents. They provide people with clear direction, substantial encouragement, personal attention, and meaningful feedback. Leaders make people feel like winners, and winning people like to continue raising the stakes!

Celebrating team accomplishments adds fun to hard work and reinforces team spirit. Celebrations increase people's network of connections and promote information sharing. Fostering high quality interpersonal relationships enhances productivity along with both physical and psychological health.

The commitments of leaders to *Encouraging the Heart* involve

- Recognizing individual contributions
- Celebrating team accomplishments

While organizing and running a day camp, one student recognized volunteers and celebrated accomplishments through her actions. She explains, "We had a pizza party with the children on the last day of the day camp. Later, the volunteers were sent thank you notes and 'valuable volunteer awards' personally signed by the day campers. The pizza party, thank you notes, and awards served to encourage the hearts of the volunteers in the hopes that they might return for next year's day camp."

4   *Student LPI* Feedback Workshop Design

In this workshop students receive feedback from the results of their *Student LPI*, then assess their strengths and note areas for improvement in their leadership skills. For those using the *Student LPI* as part of a course, this design can be easily adapted to a classroom situation.

Objectives

As a result of this session, students will be better able to

- Understand the specific behaviors and actions of exemplary leadership
- Identify their personal strengths as leaders
- Identify areas for improving their leadership practices
- Determine actions for becoming better leaders by increasing the frequency and comfort (skill) with which they engage in various leadership practices
- Plan how to share their results and learning from the LPI feedback session with others in their organization

Physical Setting

Students begin at round tables in the main seminar room for an overview lecture on the *Student LPI* and interpretation of their results. Following some individual reflection, they may cluster together in groups of two or three people for further discussion among themselves but should be together again in the main seminar room for closing comments on this session.

Materials

- Overhead transparencies
- Overhead projector and screen
- *Student LPI* Student Workbooks
- *Student LPI* feedback results for *each* participant

Group Size

Workshops using the *Student LPI* can be conducted with groups as small as four and as large as several hundred people. A group of twenty to twenty-four people is optimal, especially if only one facilitator is involved. One of the important parts of the workshop is the opportunity for students to obtain assistance from the facilitator in interpreting the *Student LPI* feedback; this should be considered when determining the size of the group and length of the workshop. The workshop includes activities for individuals, dyads or triads, and the total group.

Time Requirements

The workshop described in this manual can be conducted within as short a session as one hour or as long as four hours or even a full day, or across one or more class sessions. It can be done in the morning or the afternoon. The time varies depending on the extent to which the session is self-standing or part of a longer workshop on leadership or other management development issues. The time varies, as well, depending on whether feedback from only the Student LPI-Self is provided or Student LPI-Observer data is available, and according to how much introspection and action planning by students is desired.

Pre-Session Activities

The workshop may be designed to include completion of the *Student LPI,* or the *Student LPI* may be completed by participants prior to the workshop. If the instrument is to be administered during the workshop, a copy of the Student LPI-Self should be distributed to each student. The *Student LPI Student Workbook* contains the scoring instructions and respondent evaluation pages that will be distributed and used later in the workshop.

The *Student LPI* takes about five or ten minutes to complete. This is true for both the self and observer versions. Recording and scoring one Student LPI-Self and five Student-LPI Observers takes about 15 minutes.

The preferred option is to have students complete the Student LPI-Self prior to attending the workshop. This action heightens their interest in the workshop, where they can receive their "scores" and find out how they are doing. This interest (motivation level) is heightened when students will also be receiving feedback from other people (via the Student LPI-Observer) at the workshop. *Student LPI* data can also be collected as a pre- and post-test assessment in situations in which that is appropriate.

If a primary goal of the workshop is to help students assess their own strengths and areas for improvement as leaders, then we strongly recommend that students have the Student LPI-Observer completed by other people who interact and work with them. The combination of self-perceptions and others' perceptions greatly enhances the value of the feedback.

If they are using Student LPI-Observer forms, students should be instructed, at the time they receive their Student LPI-Self, to distribute a Student LPI-Observer to each person from whom they would like to receive feedback regarding their leadership behavior. It is preferable to solicit completion of at least five Student LPI-Observers (which allows for one or two people to not return or complete them, for whatever reason), but more observers can be invited to participate. It is not necessary to have everyone in the student leader's organization complete the Student LPI-Observer. Participants put their names on their own Student LPI-Self and each copy of the Student LPI-Observer form *before* distribution. Both the Student LPI-Self and Student LPI-Observer are typically returned directly to the facilitator to make certain that feedback will be available at the workshop for participants. This also encourages confidentiality for those returning Student LPI-Observers. We recommend that, when possible, *Student LPI* forms be returned at least one week prior to the start of the workshop or class session. This allows sufficient time for follow-up with those who have not returned their own forms or had their forms returned by others.

Important: On both the Student LPI-Self and the Student LPI-Observer forms, the information in the "Further Instructions" section on where the respondents are to return the forms should be filled out before distribution to students or observers, to avoid the forms being returned to the wrong place. Students can fill out the information for each of their Student LPI-Observer forms.

Note that the Student LPI-Observer forms are intended to be completed anonymously. This is also the preferred option when the LPI is used with managers and executives. Our studies have shown that people provide more reliable feedback when they don't have to reveal their identity to the leader (and this applies for both positive and negative reasons). The tradeoff, however, is that sometimes the leader can't completely understand the feedback, especially individual responses that are at variance with everyone else's, without knowing the source. We suggest addressing this issue directly during the feedback session with student leaders.

5 Workshop Process Details

This chapter gives step-by-step instructions for conducting a workshop on the practices of exemplary leaders. The "you" in this section refers directly to the facilitator and generally assumes little or no prior experience on his or her (your) part. Times are approximate. Some optional steps are also included. Masters for creating overhead transparencies and handouts are provided in Appendix A.

Introduction   (5–10 MINUTES)

Begin with an overview of the session and design. If the students have completed the *Student LPI* prior to the session, tell them when they will receive their feedback. If they will complete the *Student LPI* during the session, it should be completed either at this time or after you have led a discussion concerning a definition of leadership.

Discussion on Leadership   (10–15 MINUTES)

Slide

Ask: "What Is Leadership?" Seek several definitions and comments from the participants. Note their comments on newsprint.

Lead a Discussion. Discuss how management and leadership are similar and how they are different. Again, write down salient points on newsprint.

Write the Definition. After everyone has made a contribution, write the following definition of leadership on the flip chart. Explain that it will be used for the purposes of this workshop and that it was suggested by sociologist Vance Packard more than thirty-six years ago in an influential book entitled *The Pyramid Climbers:*

Leadership appears to be the art of getting others to want to do something you are convinced should be done.[17]

Look at Key Words. Suggest to the group that the key words are "want to" and ask the students to discuss how the meaning differs when these two words are left out of the definition. (People often say it is then a definition of management.)

Discuss Internal Motivation. Explain that leadership is about internal motivation (getting others to "want to" do something). Talk some more about the concept.

Cover Other Phrases. Also direct everyone's attention to other critical phrases in the definition, such as "the art" (not the science), "getting others" (not about doing it yourself), and "you are convinced" (leadership requires focus and commitment).

Write Another Definition. Next, write the following definition of leadership from *The Leadership Challenge* on the flip chart:

> The art of mobilizing others to want to struggle for shared aspirations.

Explain that of the more than two hundred definitions of leadership provided in the social science literature all are generally compatible with the Kouzes and Posner leadership practices framework, which is the conceptual foundation for the *Student LPI*.

Warm-Up   (OPTIONAL; 30–45 MINUTES)

Prepare students for a discussion of leadership by relating it to their own experiences in one of two ways:

Personal Best

Explain the Research. Explain that Kouzes and Posner researched leadership by seeking examples of the "personal-best" leadership experiences of more than 100,000 interviewees. Say that interviews were their primary means of collecting information about the times when people did their best as leaders.

Ask for Their Own Experiences. Ask students to think about a time when they have been at their personal best as leaders and to identify five to seven

17. V. Packard, *The Pyramid Climbers.* New York: McGraw-Hill, 1962, p. 170.

key practices (strategies, behaviors, actions, and so on) that made a difference in that experience. Give them five to ten minutes for reflection and to make some notes for themselves.

Form Small Groups. Put students into small groups and ask them to describe their personal-best leadership experiences to one another and to explain the practices they used that made each such a good experience.

Find Common Themes. Ask the group members to listen for the common practices among the case studies presented in their small groups and to reach consensus about five to seven key practices that made the difference across all of their individual experiences. Have each group record their observations on newsprint sheets.

Have Groups Report Their Findings. Reassemble the total group. Have small groups report their observations about the most important practices, displaying their newsprint lists.

If time permits, after all the small groups have made their presentations, have the total group identify the practices that are similar across all the small groups.

Look for Similarities. Ask the students whether there was more similarity among their key leadership practices or differences across their leadership experiences. (The answer should be overwhelmingly the former.)

Use what they have said to reinforce the notion that leadership is not something mysterious but comprises a learnable set of behaviors and skills.

Most Admired Leader

An equally powerful but somewhat less personal way of engaging students in a discussion of leadership is to ask them to think about their most admired leader. (This assignment could also be completed prior to the workshop.)

Ask the Students for Their Most-Admired Leaders. Start by asking:

Who is the person you most admire as a leader?

Encourage students to think of people they have had firsthand experience with, although some will undoubtedly select historical or contemporary public leaders.

Have Students Reflect. Have students reflect about and record their answers to the following questions:

"What does (did) this person do?" and "What qualities does this person have that make you admire her or him as a leader?"

Allow five to ten minutes for reflection and writing.

Form Small Groups. Form small groups in which each student relates to the other members the actions and qualities he or she has recorded. Tell everyone to listen for common elements and record their observations on newsprint.

Lead a Group Discussion. Bring the total group back together and have each small group give a brief report on its findings to the total group, displaying their newsprint lists. Tell the total group to look for common threads and generalizations that can be made. Discuss and list them for all to see.

Use what they have said to reinforce the notion that leadership is not something mysterious but comprises a learnable set of behaviors and skills.

Completion of the Student LPI-Self   (10 MINUTES)

If the instrument was completed before the session, skip this section.

Complete the Instrument. Following the instructions on the first page of the *Student LPI*, ask students to complete pages 2 and 3 of their instruments, but not to score them yet.

Distribute the Observer. If students have not had others complete the Observer form prior to the workshop, give them copies now so that they can ask others to complete it later and then log the results on their scoring sheets. It is also a good idea for them to ask other people to complete the Observer questionnaire in about six months, after they have had an opportunity to practice some of the behaviors they will learn in the workshop.

Lecture on the Practices of Exemplary Leadership
(20–40 MINUTES)

Give a Lecture. Before asking students to score the instrument, give a brief lecture on the practices of exemplary leadership, using overheads 1A through 1F and 2A through 2B in Appendix A and other material in this manual and in the Student Workbook. You may also expand the lecture by using material from *The Leadership Challenge*.

Provide Examples and Connections. Give as many of your own personal examples as possible, as they will be very useful in supplementing and enriching the lecture.

Also relate your presentation to the students' observations in their personal-best or most admired leader discussions, using the newsprint sheets that were created earlier.

Presentation of the *Student Leadership Practices Inventory*
(20–40 MINUTES)

Explain the Instrument. Start by presenting the following explanation to the group (Overheads 1A through 1F):

> You will be receiving feedback from yourself (and from others) about how frequently you engage in those behaviors and actions that you (in your personal-best or most admired leader discussions) and Kouzes and Posner's research (as reported in *The Leadership Challenge*) have identified as the practices and behaviors of people when they are leading and making a difference.
>
> The *Leadership Practices Inventory* was developed from the research of Kouzes and Posner on what people were doing when they were at their personal best as leaders. Kouzes and Posner translated the various actions, attitudes, tactics, and strategies into a set of statements about leadership behavior.
>
> They posed the following hypothesis:
>
> > "If this is what people say they were doing when they were at their personal best as leaders, then we should expect to find that people who engage in these behaviors are more effective and successful than people who do not engage in these behaviors."
>
> Research over the years, now involving more than 100,000 people from a wide variety of organizations, offers empirical evidence to support this view.
>
> Kouzes and Posner began extending their research to college students early on. They and their colleagues have worked with over 5,000 students, from junior high and high schools, community and junior colleges, four-year colleges and universities, and graduate schools. They spent nearly two years adapting the original LPI, which was developed for use with business and public-sector managers, into a version of the questionnaire that was appropriate for and in the language of students.
>
> The *Student LPI* has been shown in a series of studies involving student leaders to differentiate successfully between effective and less effective student leaders, not only from their own perspectives, but also from the perspectives of their constituents

(the members of their teams, clubs, or chapters or the people living on their floor or working with them in their classes) and from the perspective of their university advisers and supervisors.

Ask Whether Everyone Completed the Questionnaire. Remind students that they completed the *Student LPI,* either at the start of the session or prior to the workshop (and that they distributed copies of the Student LPI-Observer to their colleagues and had replies sent to the facilitator). Ask whether they remember completing the inventory and ask them to recall their small-group discussions about personal bests, which generated many similar observations.

Discuss the Questionnaire's Development. Say a few words (or more, depending on the interest of the group) about the development of the *Student LPI* (Overhead 3):

> The *Student LPI* contains thirty behavior-based statements. Each statement asks respondents about a specific leadership behavior and the extent to which respondents actually engage in that behavior. The *Student LPI* is not about attitudes or intentions but about actual behaviors.
>
> The *Student LPI* provides information on each of the five leadership practices identified by Kouzes and Posner's research. There are six questions for each of the five leadership practices (scales):
>
> Challenging the Process
> Inspiring a Shared Vision
> Enabling Others to Act
> Modeling the Way
> Encouraging the Heart

Briefly discuss the *reliability* and *validity* of the *Student LPI,* assuring the group that the *Student LPI* has very been thoroughly tested as a psychological instrument and is the leading leadership development instrument for use with students and that the LPI is one of the leading leadership instruments for managers and executives as well. If you wish to go into detail about the concepts of reliability and validity, you could use the following text:

Reliability

> Reliability refers to the extent to which the instrument or questionnaire contains measurement errors that cause scores to differ for reasons unrelated to the individual respondent. Reliability is determined empirically in several ways.

Internal Reliability. One way to determine reliability is to split the responses in half and test to see whether the two halves are correlated with one another. If the questionnaires were completed by the same person at the same time, we would expect responses to be reasonably consistent between the two halves. If they were perfectly independent (for example, one half is an apple, and the other half is an orange), we would expect zero correlation (although in the above example there might be some correlation, given that both items are fruits, rather than, say, a fruit and a vegetable). Should they be perfectly correlated (for example, two halves of the same apple) we would expect a 1.0 correlation coefficient. "Acceptable" scores are usually .50 or greater, and the LPI scales are generally above .66; thus the LPI has strong internal reliability.

Test-Retest Reliability. Another empirical measure of reliability is whether the instrument is overly sensitive to extraneous factors that might affect respondents' scores. For example, might the time of day, weather, individual personality, political or social events, internal organizational activity levels, or the like affect a respondent's scores from one administration of the instrument to another administration?

Over periods as short as one or two days or as long as three to four weeks, scores on the *Student LPI* show significant test-retest reliability (or consistency) at levels greater than .91 correlation. However, it should be pointed out that we would expect *Student LPI* scores to change, assuming that respondents have attended a leadership workshop (such as this one), are consciously working to change their leadership behavior, or have experienced a significant emotional life or organizational event.

Number of Items. Finally, reliability is enhanced when respondents are asked about a behavior (assessed) more than once. Therefore, a two-item scale is inherently more reliable than a one-item scale. The *Student LPI* scales each comprise *six* items or statements.

Validity

Validity is the determination of whether the instrument truly assesses what it purports to measure and also the issue of "So what? What difference does it make how I score on this instrument?" Like reliability, validity is determined in several ways.

Face Validity. The most common assessment of validity is called face validity. On the basis of subjective evaluation, does the instrument appear to be measuring what we think it is measuring? Given that the statements on the *Student LPI* are quite clearly related to the statements that you listed during the warm-up activities (personal best or most admired leader), we can say that the *Student LPI* has excellent face validity.

Empirical Measures. Validity is also determined empirically. Factor analysis is used to determine the extent to which the various instrument items are measuring common or different content areas. The results of these analyses consistently reveal that the *Student LPI* contains five factors and that the items within each factor correspond more among themselves than they do with the other factors. This means, for example, that the items that measure "Challenging the Process" are all more related (correlated) with one another than they are with items measuring the other four practices.

Predictive or Concurrent Validity. The question of "So what?" is probably the most important concern for you as workshop participants. To answer this question we look at determining predictive and/or concurrent validity, assessing the extent to which *Student LPI* scores are correlated (associated) with other important variables.

The *Student LPI* has excellent "so what?" validity, as shown by studies of the relationship between LPI scores and such variables as team cohesion, member commitment and loyalty, satisfaction, upward influence, and credibility.

For example, in studies of fraternity and sorority chapter presidents, effectiveness measured along several dimensions is positively correlated with the frequency with which these student leaders were seen as engaging in the *Student LPI* behaviors by chapter members. Resident directors reported that the most effective RAs on their campus were the ones who engaged most frequently in these leadership practices, and this was corroborated by assessments from the students living on their floors or in their facilities. New students on campus, participating in a three-day orientation session, reported levels of satisfaction that were positively correlated with the extent to which their orientation adviser engaged in these five leadership practices. Even the effectiveness of peer educators can be differentiated by the extent to which they behaved as leaders.

Overall, you can make a strong *normative* statement that those who engage in the set of behaviors described in the *Student LPI* more frequently, as opposed to less frequently, are more likely to be effective leaders. In fact, no matter where on the scale individuals initially score, to the extent that they can increase the frequency of their behavior along these dimensions, they will become more effective leaders.

If anyone has additional questions about reliability, validity, or the psychometric properties of the instrument, ask him or her to bring this up with you at the break.

Addressing Common Questions

You will want to address several questions frequently asked about the *Student LPI* (Overhead 4):

Question 1: What are the right answers?

There are no universal right answers when it comes to leadership. Still, the research indicates that the more frequently you are perceived as engaging in the behavior and actions identified in the *Student LPI,* the more likely it is that you will be perceived as an effective leader.

Question 2: How reliable and valid is the Student LPI?

Generally, this is simply another way of asking the question, "Do my scores make a difference?" The answer to the latter question is *yes,* there is a positive, direct correlation between *Student LPI* scores and effectiveness assessments. That is, as the frequency with which people are seen as engaging in the set of behaviors described on the *Student LPI* increases, so do positive assessments of such factors as their effectiveness, work group performance, team cohesiveness, credibility, and the like. Studies show that the *Student LPI* has very sound psychometric properties (which can be described more completely at the break—unless many people are interested in the research).

Question 3: Should my perceptions be consistent with the ratings other people give me?

The general answer to this question is *yes,* although there may be understandable exceptions, which we will discuss more when we look at the actual data. The usual response is that people are more effective when their self-perception matches the perception of them provided by other people.

Question 4: Can I change my leadership behavior?

To this question the answer is categorically *yes*. Leadership is a skill like any other skill, which means that with feedback, practice, and good coaching, people can improve at it. However, few people improve their skills dramatically overnight!

Scores and Interpretation of the *Student LPI*
(30–60 MINUTES)

The following steps presume that students have responses not only from their own questionnaires but also from the Student LPI-Observers. If data is available only from their own perceptions, suggest (1) that they be aware of the tendency to rate themselves more favorably than others do and (2) that the most important perceptions are those from the people whom they are trying to influence and lead. Still, much can be learned from an analysis of one's self-perceived strengths and areas for improvement.

Turn to Scoring Grids. Having explained the leadership framework and assured the students that the *Student LPI* is a valid and useful instrument, direct students to pages 12–15 in their workbooks, which are the grids for recording *Student LPI* responses. You may also show Overhead 5.

The first grid (Challenging the Process) is for recording responses for statements 1, 6, 11, 16, 21, and 26 from the Student LPI-Self and Student LPI-Observer instruments. These are the statements that relate to behaviors involved in Challenging the Process, such as searching for opportunities, experimenting and taking risks. An abbreviated form of each statement is printed beside the grid as a handy reference.

Explain the Process. Ask the students to direct their attention to you for a few minutes while you explain how to record and interpret the data. Assure the group members that they will have individual time for further study and reflection on the feedback.

Direct the students' attention to the section of the grid labeled "Self-Rating." Have them transfer their own responses to this first column. Remind them to use the columns (vertical) rather than the rows (horizontal).

Transfer Observer Scores. If others were asked to complete the Student LPI-Observer and if the forms were returned, have them enter those scores in the columns (A, B, C, D, E, and so on) under the heading "Observers' Ratings" in the same way as the "self" responses. The process is simply to transfer the numbers from page 4 of each Student LPI-Observer to the scoring grids. The grids provide space for the scores of as many as ten observers.

Total the Scores. After the students have recorded their responses for Challenging the Process, ask them to total each column and write the sums in the row marked "Totals," then to add all the totals for observers—excluding the "self" total.

Next have them enter their grand totals in the space marked "Total of All Observers' Scores."

Average the Scores. Finally, to obtain their average scores, have each student divide his or her grand total by the number of people who completed their Student LPI-Observers and write this average in the blank provided.

The sample that follows shows how the grid would look if scores for one Self and five Observers had been entered.

Sample Grid with Scores from Self and Five Observers

	SELF-RATING	OBSERVERS' RATINGS										
		A	B	C	D	E	F	G	H	I	J	
1. Seeks challenge	5	4	2	4	4	2						
6. Keeps current	4	4	3	4	4	3						
11. Initiates experiments	3	3	2	2	2	1						
16. Looks for ways to improve	4	3	2	3	5	3						
21. Asks "What can we learn?"	2	3	2	3	3	2						TOTAL OF ALL OBSERVERS' SCORES
26. Lets others take risks	5	3	3	2	3	2						
TOTALS	23	20	14	18	21	13						86

TOTAL SELF-RATING: ___23___   AVERAGE OF ALL OBSERVERS: ___17.2___

Finish the Grids. Tell students to complete the other four grids in the same manner. The second grid (Inspiring a Shared Vision) is for recording responses to the statements that pertain to envisioning the future and enlisting the support of others. These include statements 2, 7, 12, 17, 22, and 27. The third grid (Enabling Others to Act) pertains to statements 3, 8, 13, 18, 23, and 28, which involve fostering collaboration and strengthening others. The fourth grid (Modeling the Way) pertains to statements about setting an example and planning small wins. These include statements 4, 9, 14, 19, 24, and 29. The fifth grid (Encouraging the Heart) pertains to statements about recognizing contributions and celebrating accomplishments. These are statements 5, 10, 15, 20, 25, and 30.

Look at "Self" Scores. After everyone has finished recording scores, ask the students to begin to look at individual responses; remind them of the rating system that was used:

"1" means that you *rarely or seldom* engage in the behavior.
"2" means that you engage in the behavior *once in a while*.
"3" means that you *sometimes* engage in the behavior.
"4" means that you engage in the behavior *fairly often*.
"5" means that you engage in the behavior *very frequently*.

Have students begin to interpret their responses by examining their self-ratings. On each completed grid, have them look at their responses in the blanks marked "Total Self-Rating." Each of these totals represents the students' own responses to six statements about one of the five leadership practices. Each total can range from a low of 6 to a high of 30.

Ask the students to write "1" to the left of the leadership practice with the highest total self-rating (in the "Self" column on p. 17 of their workbooks), "2" by the next-highest total self-rating, and so on (Overhead 6). Explain that this ranking represents the leadership practice with which he or she feels most comfortable, second-most comfortable, and so on.

Look at Observer Scores. Refer the students to the numbers in the blanks marked "Average of All Observers" on each grid. The number in each blank is the average score given by the people asked to complete the Student LPI-Observer. Like each total self-rating, this number can range from 6 to 30.

Have the students write "1" to the right of the leadership practice with the highest score (in the "Observers'" column on p. 17 of their workbooks), "2" by the next-highest score, and so on. Explain that this ranking represents the leadership practice that others feel the student uses most often, second-most often, and so on.

Compare Self with Observer Rankings. Continue by asking students to next look at the relationship between the rank order of their self-ratings and the ratings of their observers. Tell them to think about the extent to which their self-perceptions are consistent with the perceptions of the people with whom they work and interact. Explain that you want them to disregard their absolute scores for a moment and to reflect on the match (or mismatch) between "self" and "observer" perceptions of "reality" (in terms of leadership).

Ask students:

> Which of these two columns (A = Self or B = Observer) is the better representation of *reality*? If I didn't know you, but only had the *Student LPI* scores provided by you and by other people who had interacted with you, whose scores would I consider to be the best representation of how you actually behave?

The response from participants will generally be "the scores or assessments of others," and this is true. (That is why it is important to look at the degree of agreement between the two rank orderings. Even though there may be differences between the absolute scores from the Self and Observer columns [that is, "23" is not the same as "17.2"], it is possible that both parties will agree on the rank order of this practice, indicating agreement on the strength of this leadership behavior versus the others.)

Look at Each Question. Point out the columns marked with the letters "A," "B," "C," "D," and so on, noting that these represent the actual responses on the five practices from each person who completed the Student LPI-Observer. Tell the students that this gives them an overall assessment of their leadership practices as seen by each individual Student LPI-Observer respondent. Ask them to note where there is agreement and disagreement among these respondents about their strengths and areas for improvement in these leadership practices (Overhead 5). Add the following:

> The Student LPI-Observer respondents are not individually identified on your sheets. People often wish they knew exactly who these individuals were so that they could better understand the feedback. Resist the desire to figure out the identities of particular individuals; it is more important that you understand what this person or these people are trying to tell you. In any case, earlier research has indicated that participants were only about 25 percent successful in matching names with scores.
>
> The tradeoff is generally between identification (nonconfidentiality) of respondents and quality of data. Student LPI-Observer respondents are more likely to give better (more honest, more candid) responses—positive as well as negative—when they don't have to worry about being identified. Kouzes and Posner have designed the questionnaires to obtain the higher quality data. At the end of the workshop, several strategies will be offered to help you collect more data and find out more about people's opinions of your leadership effectiveness.

Graph the Scores. To compare Student LPI-Self and Student LPI-Observer assessments, refer students to the "Chart for Graphing Your Scores" on page 19 of their workbooks. You may also want to do an example on Overhead 7 so that students can see what you are talking about. They can also refer to the example on page 18 of their workbooks. Instruct the students to designate self-ratings in the five leadership practices (Challenging, Inspiring, Enabling, Modeling, and Encouraging) by marking each of these points with a capital "S" (for "Self") and then to connect the five resulting "S scores" with a *solid line* and to label the end of this line "Self." Next, have students designate the average observer scores by marking each of the points with a capital letter "O" (for "Observer"), connecting the five resulting "O scores" with a *dashed line,* and labeling the end of this line "Observer."

Each student will now have a graphic representation (one solid and one dashed line) illustrating the relationship between his or her self-perception and the observations of other people.

- Direct their attention to how parallel the two lines are—indicating relative agreement about both strengths and areas for improvement.
- Point out that if there are significant gaps between self and observer ratings that these indicate areas for improvement.

Explain Percentiles. On the "Chart for Graphing Your Scores," explain the column marked "Percentile." Say that percentiles represent the scores nation-wide from students who have completed the *Student LPI* (over 1,200).[18] Give the following explanation:

> Because scores are *normally distributed* (in the classic bell-shaped curve), most people's scores fall at the fiftieth percentile (roughly half of the scores fall above and roughly half of the scores fall below) and nearly two-thirds of all scores fall within one standard deviation of the mean.
>
> A percentile ranking is determined by the percentage of people who score at or below a given number. For example, if a person's total self-rating for "Challenging" is at the sixtieth percentile line on the chart, this means that this person assessed himself or herself higher than 60 percent of all people who have completed the *Student LPI;* this person ranked himself or herself in the top 40 percent in this leadership practice. Studies indicate that a "high" score is one at or above the seventieth percentile, a "low" score is one at or below the thirtieth percentile, and a score that falls between those ranges is considered "moderate."

---

18. The percentile scores represent only those from the Student LPI-Self.

Compare Scores with Those of Other Student Leaders. Ask the students, using these criteria, to circle the "H" (for "High"), the "M" (for "Moderate"), or the "L" (for "Low") for each leadership practice in the "Range of Scores" table on page 20 of their workbooks (Overhead 8). Have them compare their leadership scores with those of other student leaders around the country. (Remember that, given a normal distribution, it is expected that most people's scores will fall within the moderate range.)

Give students a few moments to compare themselves normatively with other students across the country. While this is interesting (and often requested by students), point out that this comparison does not necessarily say much about leadership for any particular person in any specific organization or organizational context. Explain by saying:

> Because leadership is a skill, you will want to determine what it
> will take for you to improve your base level of leadership abil-
> ity regardless of where you are relative to others.

Fill in Workbooks. Thus far you have been asking students to complete the analysis while you have been describing it. In a few moments you will give them some additional time to review the individual items on the *Student LPI* and to look more deeply at individual responses and specific items. What you want to do now is just explain where in their workbooks they can make notes to themselves as they continue their analysis.

To facilitate individual assessment and interpretations, ask the students to look at pages 21–22 in their workbooks. Tell them that this space is provided for them to make notes to themselves about the *specific behaviors* within each leadership practice. For example, sometimes a student's score on a leadership practice may be high or low because *all* the specific behaviors were assessed as frequently, or as not frequently, engaged in. Other times the score may be influenced by only a single behavior or a few behaviors connected with a leadership practice. Here is where they can make notes about the specific behaviors that make up the various leadership practices.

For those students with data from Observers, page 23 provides space to note areas of agreement and disagreement between their self perceptions and the perceptions of others. They may also note inconsistencies between the assessments of their observers, as well as areas of agreement.

When they have completed this analysis, tell the students to summarize their findings by completing the Strengths and Opportunities Summary Worksheet on page 26 of their workbooks (Overhead 9). Having completed the item-by-item analysis, looked at their own assessments in comparison with those provided by others, charted their scores against student leaders from across the country, and so on, they should be able to say about themselves: "Here's what I do well (or comfortably)" and "here's an area where I could improve my leadership ability."

Provide students with sufficient time for both this analysis and summary. You can either have everyone in the group work until a specific time (or in the case of a class, this assignment could be taken home), and then provide instructions for completing the Action-Planning Worksheet (Overhead 11, more details follow), or you can include instructions for action plans along with the preceding explanation for pages 21–26 of the Student Workbook.

If you haven't taken a break yet, this is a perfect place to do so, and it is also a logical place to break if you are doing the Student LPI *over more than one session.*

Make Action Plans. Start by offering students some ideas for moving from analysis to action. Use the "Prescriptions for Meeting the Leadership Challenge" (Overhead 10), which is on page 27 of their workbooks. There are ten ideas, two for each leadership practice, that are quick ways to start. Say a word or two about each prescription, providing an example or illustration. Depending on time, you could also brainstorm with the entire group about additional ideas or break the students into small discussion groups to generate ideas and then share them.

In Appendix B of this facilitator's guide there are checklists with a number of other suggestions for how students can improve their skills relative to each leadership practice. These can be used in several ways:

- Make copies of the suggestions as a handout for students and distribute them prior to their action planning or later as further suggestions.
- Use these ideas to supplement students' own brainstorming about how to improve their capabilities in these leadership practices.

Note: We find it helpful to ask students to put a check mark by each idea that they think they could do *right away*. Then we suggest that students select one or two of the ideas that they checked and complete the Action-Planning Worksheet for how they will put these suggestions into practice in their organization (or club, group, team, community, project). Although students can use these prescriptions immediately, you might suggest instead that they use these ten ideas as a starting point for brainstorming other ideas that will make more sense for them in their own circumstances.

- Add some of these to the ideas aired in the small group discussions about "What Works for Me" (see the next section).
- Make overhead transparencies of the checklists in Appendix B, and have students identify the items they think would be most useful, suggest variations on the ideas, and ask questions about how to implement any of the suggestions.

Encourage Action Planning. Once you've finished "priming the pump" by giving students some ideas for how they can be even better leaders than they are today, ask them to complete the Action-Planning Worksheet on pages 28–29 of the Student Workbook (Overhead 11). Encourage students to select at least one leadership practice or behavior that they believe they can improve and to create an action plan for doing so. The Action-Planning Worksheets also can be completed as a take-home assignment following the workshop or class or used as the basis for a follow-up leadership-development program. (*Note:* The Student Workbooks contain one Action-Planning Worksheet. Students can copy the blank before filling it in, or just use separate sheets of paper to develop an action plan for each practice they want to improve.

Dyad or Triad Work (10–30 MINUTES, OR AS MUCH AS 90 MINUTES IF THE OPTIONAL ACTIVITY IS USED)

Students often find it helpful to share their scores with one another and to ask their peers for assistance in interpreting them. Peers often see messages not readily perceived by the recipient of the feedback. This peer exchange also helps students become more comfortable with openly discussing their strengths and areas for improvement. Going public increases ownership of the data and prepares them for back-home discussions they might wish to have with their constituents.

Hold Small-Group Discussions. Suggest that as people finish up their individual reflections they form small groups (perhaps at their tables) of two or three people.

Ask the groups to discuss what sense they made of their feedback—what it told them about themselves, what actions they think they could take to improve themselves, and what information they wish they had to help them understand their *Student LPI* feedback.

Consider the Data. Following this discussion, provide students with a few more minutes to revisit their notes and make any additions based on any new input from the small group. They may also have some additional questions and insights they want to bring up with the entire group.

Optional Small-Group Activity   (20-30 MINUTES)

After providing students the opportunity to process their own data (which may or may not include completing the Action-Planning Worksheets), you may want them to think more about their leadership strengths and come up with suggestions for others.

Form Groups. Either put students into groups based on their most or second-most frequent leadership practice score or, if you have access to the student's leadership practice scores prior to the workshop, assign them to one of the five leadership practice groups. (This can also be done on a random assignment basis. Everyone has something to contribute for each leadership practice, even the one they claim to be the least comfortable or skillful with.)

Try to make the groups approximately equal in number of members. Keep the five breakout groups together in one room or assign them to different locations. (Or give them this assignment to take home and come back with their reports at another time.)

Assign a Task. Ask the members of each group to think about "what works for me" when it comes to using the particular leadership practice assigned to their group. (See the checklists in Appendix B, which can be used as overhead transparencies or as handouts.)

Have people take a few moments to jot down four or five ideas individually about how they use this leadership practice. Encourage people to be as specific as possible with their ideas, giving examples whenever they can.

When everyone has finished, have each group member share one idea from his or her list within the small group, continuing until all the ideas from each person are "in the air" (or "on the table"). The group members may want to talk more about these ideas with one another.

Have each group develop a list of eight to ten of their best ideas and write these on newsprint sheets or on an overhead transparency. Tell them that these are the ideas and suggestions the group would offer to others who want to be more effective in using this leadership practice.

After the groups come up with their lists, have them put stars (or asterisks) by their two *best ideas,* which they will present orally to everyone else in the workshop. Make sure they choose spokespeople for their groups.

Present Ideas. Reassemble the five groups into one group. It doesn't matter which order the leadership practices are presented or discussed in (which is another observation about leadership that can be made).

Have each group post its entire list of ideas for its particular leadership practice and then have the spokesperson from each group explain its two best ideas to everyone else and provide examples of how to implement them (for those who may be less comfortable in doing so, or who may not know how).

Tell each spokesperson to think of his or her job in this presentation as coaching the rest of the group (or workshop participants or class) on how to become more comfortable and effective in using this leadership practice. The goal is that everyone in the workshop will end up with a number of very practical ideas for improving their leadership abilities.

Record the Results. When each spokesperson is done, ask if anyone in his or her group wants to make any additional comments or if anyone in any of the other groups has any questions or needs any clarification (for example, sometimes something else will be written on the newsprint that needs an explanation). (*Note*: The checklists in Appendix B can also be handed out at this point.)

After the five group presentations (one for each leadership practice), the newsprint sheets from this exercise can be collected, transcribed (typed and formatted), and copied to be given to participants for their leadership "tool kits."

(If the exercise is given as a take-home assignment, instruct each group to bring sufficient copies of its newsprint or overhead transparency or Powerpoint® presentation for everyone else in the workshop or class.)

Wrap Up the Discussion. Following the presentations, give students some time to make notes about the lessons learned from this coaching session. Ask them:

What else can you do to be an even better leader?

The LPI Feedback Back Home   (OPTIONAL; 10–20 MINUTES)

This section presumes that feedback from the Student LPI-Observer is available.

Think Ahead. Remind students that leadership is a relationship—that without constituents there is no leader—and explain that one of the most important ways to benefit from the *Student LPI* feedback is to share both the results and tentative interpretations with the people who provided or generated the data in the first place.

To reinforce the importance of students incorporating the *Student LPI* feedback into their back-home lives, have them think for a few minutes about how they are going to share their feedback, interpretation, and action plans with their constituents.

Explain that these people can also help to clarify ambiguous or inconsistent scores and that gaining their support will make any leadership development effort that much more painless and any experiments more likely to be successful.

Gain Commitment. Accomplish the first step in this process by having all participants make a commitment to hold such a feedback session with their constituents following the workshop. Have each student choose a time when he or she will hold such a meeting (even if it is one-on-one) and whom he or she will invite to attend and participate in the dialogue.

Confirm in Writing. If time permits, have students actually write out what they will say to others about what they have learned, what they were delighted or surprised about, what they plan to do in the future, and the like.

Tell the students that what they do in their back-home situations with the information they have about their leadership styles is an important opportunity to put the entire leadership model that they have been learning about into practice. Tell them the following:

> Since most of us, especially those in leadership positions, don't typically share feedback with others, the act of doing so is an example of our willingness to *Challenge the Process* by experimenting and taking a risk. In having this conversation, you also create an opportunity to *Inspire a Shared Vision* by talking about the things that are most important to you (vision and values) and to your organization (or club, team, etc.) and both why and how these things are important to everyone in the organization as well. By letting others know that their opinions are taken seriously, you are *Enabling Others to Act* and underscoring how competent and influential you find others to be. Handling constructive criticism as well as praise when you discuss your leadership style with others requires *Modeling the Way*, and this session is but the first step (small win) in becoming an even better leader. Finally, you can *Encourage the Heart*—provide donuts and coffee for the discussion!
>
> Moreover, within this session (which might be facilitated by a third party such as a faculty or student services adviser), you can gain considerable insight into how your actions are perceived (perhaps differently from how they are intended) and ideas about what others believe you could be doing more of, better, or even less of ("stop doing . . .").
>
> Ask for help from other students in the group in accomplishing some of these tasks and discuss the actions of group members that dis-enable them from being better leaders.

Dispel Fears. If students are uncomfortable with the thought of reviewing their *Student LPI* feedback in a group setting, encourage them to consider doing this one-on-one or with small clusters of people, beginning with those with whom they have the best relationships.

Workshop Closing   (5 MINUTES)

As you bring the workshop to closure, you have an important opportunity not only to summarize what has gone on but to encourage students to continue to take on the *challenge* of being leaders and of being even better leaders than they have been. Share some of the following observations and add your own hints to help and encourage students to develop into exemplary leaders:

No single instrument is a perfect measure or a perfect predictor of behavior. Although the *Student LPI* is a valid and reliable inventory, it does not describe the entire universe of leadership. Continually seek other useful, valid, and reliable sources of feedback.

The best way to find out what others mean by the scores or ratings they gave is to ask them. Rather than trying to second-guess the people who have completed the Student LPI-Observer for you, have one-on-one discussions with each of these people or arrange a group meeting to openly discuss the scores and ask for information on why certain responses were given. Doing so requires a certain degree of trust between you and your constituents, but if that trust exists, these discussions are the most beneficial way of finding out additional information about your leadership practices and effectiveness.

Leadership development is self-development. Leaders are their own instruments—their success and effectiveness depend on how finely tuned and well practiced they are. The only way to become a better leader is to participate continually and actively in your own development.

6

Design and Follow-Up Options

Use the Student LPI-Observer

If students have not yet done so, encourage them to use the Student LPI-Observer to gather feedback on other people's perceptions of their leadership practices. The perceptions of other people can be invaluable to students making developmental plans as leaders. Students who have already solicited feedback from members of their organizations can gather data from people outside of their organizations—alumni, university officials, and faculty, as well as peers who are in comparable positions.

Collect Open-Ended Feedback

Attach an open-ended feedback sheet to the Student LPI-Observer to allow students to gather more prescriptive information specific to their own situations. Respondents who are concerned about anonymity can usually prepare their feedback on a personal computer and print out an unidentifiable response page. Following are examples of questions that have been used for the open-ended section:

- Looking back over the individual statements in the Student LPI, which five behaviors do you wish this person would engage in more frequently? Please list them by number. Why are these important?
- Think about how you would describe this person's characteristics (values, traits, attributes) to someone else. What adjectives would you use?
- How might this person be able to improve his or her abilities to lead?

Offer Additional Workshops

Offer a workshop on each of the five leadership practices. Students can select those practices they would like to improve and participate in the relevant workshop. With assistance, student leaders might also take responsibility for designing and facilitating such additional workshops.

Have a Team-Building Session

Offer a team-building session that includes members of the students' organizations. The student leaders can use their feedback on the *Student LPI* as a portion of the meeting. The whole team could be asked to complete the Student LPI-Observer and discuss its perceptions with the student leader, or a team-building session can be designed around the ideas contained in *The Leadership Challenge*.

Show The Leadership Challenge Videos

Several videos are available that can be used in the *Student LPI* feedback workshop or subsequent workshops to illustrate the five key leadership practices.

- *The Leadership Challenge* video (about 23 minutes) provides an overview of the Kouzes-Posner leadership model and presents four case studies illustrating the leadership practices in action: Gayle Hamilton (Pacific Gas & Electric), Deborah Kaufmann (Norton Company), Ed Myers (UCLA Mail Services), and Phil Turner (Raychem). (Video available through Jossey-Bass Publishers, (800) 274-4434.)
- The video *Leadership in Action* (about 15 minutes) looks at the personal-best leadership experience of one manager (Bill Spencer). It takes the viewer through a case study at DuPont (with interviews of both the leader and his constituents) and demonstrates how the leader used the five key practices to achieve the extraordinary. (Video available through CRM Films, (800) 421-0833.)

Form Developmental Partnerships

Ask students to form partnerships of two or three people and set an agenda for where they would like to go next in their development as leaders. As partners, students are expected to support one another in their efforts, both through encouragement and counsel. A number of interesting and practical developmental suggestions are provided at the end of Chapters 3 through 12 in *The Leadership Challenge*. (A free Instructor's Guidebook is available from Jossey-Bass for those using *The Leadership Challenge* in a classroom setting.) Ask each member of the partnership to make a commitment to complete one or two developmental actions within the month following the workshop and have partners set a specific date to meet again to review their progress, learn from one another's efforts, and celebrate their accomplishments.

RECOMMENDED READINGS

Challenging the Process

Calvert, G. (1993). *Highwire management: Risk-taking tactics for leaders, innovators, and trailblazers.* San Francisco: Jossey-Bass.

Csikszentmihalyi, M. (1990). *Flow: The psychology of optimal experience.* New York: HarperCollins.

Jaffe, D. T., Scott, C. D., & Tobe, G. R. (1994). *Rekindling commitment: How to revitalize yourself, your work, and your organization.* San Francisco: Jossey-Bass.

Kanter, R. M. (1983). *The change masters: Innovation for productivity in the American corporation.* New York: Simon & Schuster.

Kriegel, R. & Patler, L. (1991). *If it ain't broke . . . break it!* New York: Warner.

Peters, T. (1992). *Liberation management: Necessary disorganization for the nanosecond nineties.* New York: Knopf.

Inspiring a Shared Vision

Bennis, W., & Nanus, B. (1985). *Leaders: The strategies for taking charge.* New York: HarperCollins.

Hamel, G., & Prahalad, C. K. (1994). *Competing for the future: Breakthrough strategies for seizing control of your industry and creating the markets of tomorrow.* Boston: Harvard Business School Press.

Nanus, B. (1992). *Visionary leadership: Creating a compelling sense of direction for your organization.* San Francisco: Jossey-Bass.

Pearce, T. (1995). *Leading out loud.* San Francisco: Jossey-Bass.

Peck, M. S. (1978). *The road less traveled.* New York: Simon & Schuster.

Quigley, J. V. (1993). *Vision: How leaders develop it, share it and sustain it.* New York: McGraw-Hill.

Schwartz, F. (1991). *The art of the long view.* New York: Currency.

Wheatley, M. (1991). *Leadership and the new science.* San Francisco: Berrett-Koehler.

Enabling Others to Act

Block, P. (1987). *The empowered manager: Positive political skills at work.* San Francisco: Jossey-Bass.

Case, J. (1995). *Open-book management: The coming business revolution.* New York: HarperCollins.

Fisher, R., & Ury, W. (1981). *Getting to yes.* Boston: Houghton-Mifflin.

Hakim, C. (1994). *We are all self-employed.* San Francisco: Berrett-Koehler.

Helgesen, S. (1995). *The web of inclusion.* New York: Currency.

Lawler, E. E., III. (1992). *The ultimate advantage: Creating the high-involvement organization.* San Francisco: Jossey-Bass.

Pffefer, J. (1994). *Competitive advantage through people: Unleashing the power of the work force.* Boston: Harvard Business School Press.

Stack, J. (1992). *The great game of business: The only sensible way to run a company.* New York: Currency.

Tannen, D. (1994). *Talking from 9 to 5: How women's and men's conversational styles affect who gets heard, who gets credit, and what gets done at work.* New York: William Morrow.

Wellins, R. E., Byham, W. C., & Wilson, J. M. (1991). *Empowered teams: Creating self-directed work groups that improve quality, productivity, and participation.* San Francisco: Jossey-Bass.

Modeling the Way

Armstrong, D. (1992). *Managing by storying around: A new method of leadership.* New York: Currency.

Collins, J., & Porras, J. (1994). *Built to last: Successful habits of visionary companies.* New York: HarperCollins.

DePree, M. (1989). *Leadership as an art.* New York: Doubleday.

DePree, M. (1992). *Leadership jazz.* New York: Doubleday.

Kouzes, J. M., & Posner, B. Z. (1993). *Credibility: How leaders gain and lose it, why people demand it.* San Francisco: Jossey-Bass.

Schultz, H. (1997). *Pour your heart into it.* New York: Hyperion.

Schwarzkopf, H. N., with Pietre, P. (1992). *It doesn't take a hero.* New York: Bantam.

Encouraging the Heart

Blanchard, K., & Bowles, S. (1998). *Gung ho!* New York: Morrow.

Deal, T. E., & Jenkins, W. A. (1994). *Managing the hidden organization: Strategies for empowering your behind-the-scenes employees.* New York: Warner.

Kohn, A. (1993). *Punished by rewards.* Boston: Houghton-Mifflin.

Kouzes, J. M., & Posner, B. Z. (1998). *Encouraging the heart: A leader's guide to rewarding and recognizing others.* San Francisco: Jossey-Bass.

Nelson, B. (1994). *1001 ways to reward employees.* New York: Workman.

Peterson, C., & Bossio, L. M. (1991). *Health and optimism: New research on the relationship between positive thinking and physical well-being.* New York: Free Press.

Seligman, M. (1990). *Learned optimism.* New York: Knopf.

Vroom, V. H. (1994). *Work and motivation.* San Francisco: Jossey-Bass.

Other Books on Leadership

Bass, B. M., & Stodgill, R. M. (1990). *Bass & Stodgill's handbook of leadership.* New York: Free Press.

Bennis, W. (1989). *On becoming a leader.* Reading, MA: Addison-Wesley.

Gardner, H. (1995). *Leading minds.* New York: HarperCollins.

Gardner, J. (1989). *On leadership.* New York: Free Press.

Heifetz, R. A. (1994). *Leadership without easy answers.* Cambridge, MA: Belknap.

Peters, T., & Austin, N. (1983). *A passion for excellence: The leadership difference.* New York: Random House.

APPENDIX A

Masters for Overhead Transparencies and Handouts

The following pages are intended to be used as masters in creating transparencies for an overhead projector. The numbers on these masters (Overhead 1A, 2A, and so on) correspond to those that appear in Chapter 5, *Workshop Process Details,* and Appendix D, which give you instructions about when and how to use these overheads in explaining the *Student LPI* and the computer-generated feedback reports.

Permission is hereby granted to project these overheads in workshops where the *Student LPI* is used and to photocopy the overheads for use as handouts to participants in such workshops.

The copyright line that appears at the bottom of each master must appear on all transparencies and handouts.

The Five Practices of Exemplary Leadership

 Challenging the Process

 Inspiring a Shared Vision

 **Enabling Others to Act**

Modeling the Way

Encouraging the Heart

Challenging the Process

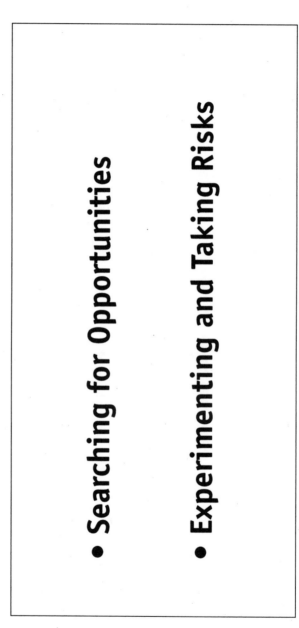

- **Searching for Opportunities**

- **Experimenting and Taking Risks**

Inspiring a Shared Vision

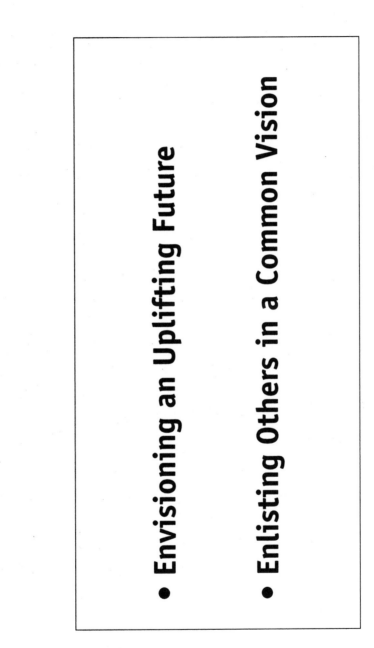

- **Envisioning an Uplifting Future**

- **Enlisting Others in a Common Vision**

 # Enabling Others to Act

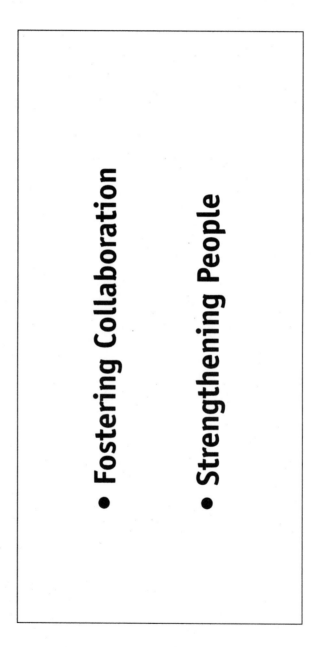

- **Fostering Collaboration**
- **Strengthening People**

✳ Modeling the Way

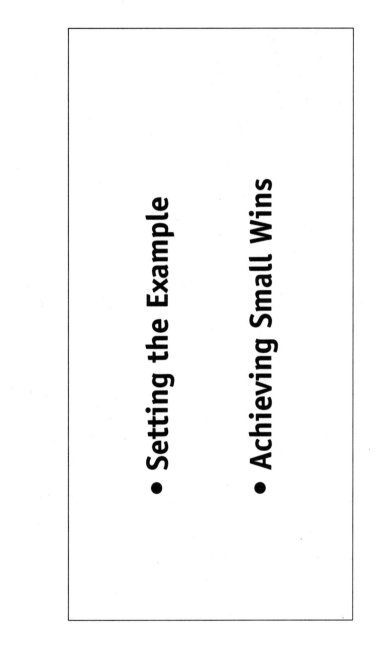

- **Setting the Example**

- **Achieving Small Wins**

★ Encouraging the Heart

- **Recognizing Individual Contributions**

- **Celebrating Team Accomplishments**

The Ten Commitments of Leadership

1. **SEARCH** for challenging opportunities to change, grow, innovate, and improve.

2. **EXPERIMENT,** take risks, and learn from the accompanying mistakes.

3. **ENVISION** an uplifting and ennobling future.

4. **ENLIST** others in a common vision by appealing to their values, interests, hopes, and dreams.

The Ten Commitments of Leadership

5. **FOSTER** collaboration by promoting cooperative goals and building trust.

6. **STRENGTHEN** people by giving power away, providing choice, developing competence, assigning critical tasks, and offering visible support.

7. **SET** the example by behaving in ways that are consistent with shared values.

8. **ACHIEVE** small wins that promote consistent progress and build commitment.

9. **RECOGNIZE** individual contributions to the success of every project.

10. **CELEBRATE** team accomplishment regularly.

Student Leadership Practices Inventory

- Based on case studies of student leaders

- 30 *behavior-based* statements

- 5 key practices (with 6 statements each)

  1. Challenging the Process
  2. Inspiring a Shared Vision
  3. Enabling Others to Act
  4. Modeling the Way
  5. Encouraging the Heart

- 5-point response scale ("5" = very frequently)

- Strong reliability and validity

Questions Frequently Asked About the *Student LPI*

1. What are the right answers?

2. How reliable and valid is the *Student LPI*?

3. Should my perceptions be consistent with the ratings other people give me?

4. Can I change my leadership behavior?

Sample Grid with Scores from Self and Five Observers

Challenging the Process

	SELF-RATING	A	B	C	D	E	F	G	H	I	J	TOTAL OF ALL OBSERVERS' SCORES
1. Seeks challenge	5	4	2	4	4	2						
6. Keeps current	4	4	3	4	4	3						
11. Initiates experiments	3	3	2	2	2	1						
16. Looks for ways to improve	4	3	2	3	5	3						
21. Asks "What can we learn?"	2	3	2	3	3	2						
26. Lets others take risks	5	3	3	2	3	2						
TOTALS	23	20	14	18	21	13					86	

OBSERVERS' RATINGS

TOTAL SELF-RATING: ___23___

AVERAGE OF ALL OBSERVERS: ___17.2___

Self

___ Challenging the Process

___ Inspiring a Shared Vision

___ Enabling Others to Act

___ Modeling the Way

___ Encouraging the Heart

Observers

___

___

___

___

___

Chart for Graphing Your Scores

Percentile	Challenging the Process	Inspiring a Shared Vision	Enabling Others to Act	Modeling the Way	Encouraging the Heart
100%	30	30	30	30	30
	29			29	
	28	29		28	
					29
	27	28			
			29		
				27	
90%	26	27			
					28
	25		28	26	
		26			
80%					27
	24	25	27	25	
					26
70%					
		24		24	
	23		26		
					25
60%		23			
				23	
	22				
					24
50%		22	25		
				22	
	21	21			23
40%			24		
		20		21	22
30%	20				
		19	23		21
				20	
20%	19	18	22	19	20
	18	17	21		19
10%	17	16	20	18	18
	16	15	19	17	17
	15	14	18	16	16

Range of Scores

In my perception				
Practice	**Rating**			
Challenging the Process	H	M	L	
Inspiring a Shared Vision	H	M	L	
Enabling Others to Act	H	M	L	
Modeling the Way	H	M	L	
Encouraging the Heart	H	M	L	

In others' perception				
Practice	**Rating**			
Challenging the Process	H	M	L	
Inspiring a Shared Vision	H	M	L	
Enabling Others to Act	H	M	L	
Modeling the Way	H	M	L	
Encouraging the Heart	H	M	L	

Strengths and Opportunities
Summary Worksheet

Strengths

Which of the leadership practices and behaviors are you most comfortable with? Why? Can you do more?

Areas for Improvement

What can you do to use a practice more frequently? What will it take to feel more comfortable?

Prescriptions for Meeting the Leadership Challenge

 Challenge the Process
- Fix something
- Adopt the "great ideas" of others

 **Inspire a Shared Vision**
- Let others know how you feel
- Recount your "personal best"

 Enable Others to Act
- Always say "we"
- Make heroes of other people

 Model the Way
- Lead by example
- Create opportunities for small wins

 Encourage the Heart
- Write "thank you" notes
- Celebrate, and link your celebrations to your organization's values

Action-Planning Worksheet

1. What would you like to be better able to do?

2. What specific actions will you take?

3. What is the *first* action you will take?
   Who will be involved? When will you begin?

   Action

   People Involved

   Target Date

4. Complete this sentence: "I will know I have improved in this leadership skill when . . . ."

5. When will you review your progress?

APPENDIX B

Checklists of Actions for Meeting
the Leadership Challenge

Checklist for Challenging the Process

_____ Volunteer for a tough assignment. Be proactive in looking for chances to stretch yourself and learn something new.

_____ Make a list of every task you perform. About each, ask yourself "Why am I doing this? Why am I doing it this way? Can this task be eliminated or done significantly better?"

_____ Make a list of all the things you do in your organization (or club, team, group, program, community) that fit this description: "That's the way we've always done things around here." For each of these, ask yourself, "How useful is this practice to doing our best?" If the answer is "absolutely essential," then keep it. Otherwise, find a way to change it.

_____ Hold a meeting with your teammates. Ask them what really annoys or bugs them about this organization. Commit to changing three of the most frequently mentioned items that are hindering success.

_____ Identify a process in your group that's not working. Whatever it is, take action to fix it.

_____ Try one or two experiments (doing something that you are not currently doing). Make them small but see what you can learn from them for future experiments (and eventually new practices).

_____ Eliminate "fire hosing" (throwing water on every new spark of an idea). Bring squirt guns to your meetings, and use them whenever someone puts down a new idea ("that'll never work") without giving it the benefit of some discussion and reflection.

_____ Go shopping for ideas. Call your counterparts in another organization, at another school, or in another community, and find out what they are doing. Better yet, go visit them in person (and take some others with you). Find one or more things that they are doing very well that your organization could and should copy. Then follow through.

_____ Read biographies about a couple of revolutionaries in business, science, politics, religion, or any endeavor. Learn whatever you can from the accounts of their lives.

_____ Identify a couple of successful people on your campus or in your community who excel at taking risks and experimenting. Interview them about what they think are the ingredients for innovation. Ask them how they get away with "breaking the rules."

_____ Take a class in creative problem solving.

_____ Spend time in an Outward Bound or similar wilderness-adventure program.

_____ Eliminate the phrase, "That's the way we did it last year" from your discussions. Review annual projects and programs to improve, change, or confirm how you are proceeding.

⚡ Checklist for Inspiring a Shared Vision

_____ Envision yourself one year from now. Write an article about how you've made a difference. Imagine that your organization (or club, team, group, community, project) has been named the outstanding group on campus. When you stand up at the award ceremony, what will you say about what you've done and why you did it?

_____ Ask yourself "Am I in this position *to do something*, or am I in it *for something to do*?" If your answer is "to do something"—then write down what you want to accomplish while you are in your current position, and why.

_____ Visualize the possibilities. Focus on all the things that could happen, not just the things that could go wrong.

_____ Write several positive affirmations: for example, "I'm confident that I'm finding opportunities as I accept these new challenges" or "I'm learning from my mistakes as I experiment with new ways to do things better."

_____ Meet with the people in your organization and ask them to talk about their hopes and aspirations for what this organization could be accomplishing. Make those common goals visible.

_____ Speak positively. Don't say *try*, say *will*. Sure, there are lots of reasons why this or that might not happen, and of course it will be hard work, but people don't get charged up when you're tentative and noncommittal.

_____ Make the intangible tangible. Slogans, theme songs, poetry, symbols, quotations, and humor are powerful tools you can use to express the values and vision of your organization.

_____ Whenever possible, volunteer to stand in front of a group and speak, even if it's just to introduce someone or make an announcement.

_____ Visit your local library, or go to a store that sells CDs, tapes, and videos. Check out or buy and then listen to several famous speeches by leaders who have been inspirational. Learn everything you can from the masters.

_____ Take a public speaking class. Join Toastmasters (a community-based organization that helps people become more comfortable speaking in public and expressing their ideas in a supportive atmosphere).

_____ Identify a couple of successful people on your campus or in your community who are good public speakers or who are inspirational to you. Interview these people about how they developed their communication skills. What's the source of their own inspiration?

_____ Use team-building activities to energize people on your team and to build interpersonal trust among participants through shared experiences.

Checklist for Enabling Others to Act

_____ Find ways to increase interaction among people in your organization (or club, group, unit, team, class, program, community) who need to work more effectively together. Have a potluck dinner. Teamwork and trust can be built only when people interact informally as well as formally.

_____ Establish easily accessible meeting areas that encourage people to interact. Locate the coffee pot, popcorn maker, or microwave oven between people who should talk with one another.

_____ For the next two weeks, commit to replacing the word "I" with "we." Leadership is a team effort, not an individual effort. "We" is an inclusive word that signals a commitment to teamwork and sharing. Use it liberally.

_____ Assign important tasks to others. Don't always hog the limelight. Let someone else make a key presentation. Coach and support that person.

_____ Ask for volunteers. Give people choices. You build commitment when people don't feel forced into taking action. You build motivation when people feel like they're in control.

_____ Keep your door open all the time (except when you must discuss an extremely private personnel matter). Closed doors send a signal that you don't want to interact with others, breeding distrust and suspicion.

_____ Remove unnecessary steps in any approval process.

_____ Interview an athletic coach. Ask how you might apply the coach's methods in your organization. What does it mean to "coach"?

_____ Choose someone on your campus or in your community who's known as an exceptional "people person." Accompany and observe this person for a few hours. Ask for tips on how you can do better.

_____ Study a social movement (for example, civil rights or women's suffrage), and find out how proponents encouraged others to get involved.

_____ Take a course in team building or a class on listening skills, consulting skills, or running effective meetings.

_____ Mentor new members in your organization. Pair experienced leaders with emerging leaders.

_____ Make people visible by connecting them directly with your group's key stakeholders (such as faculty, administrators, alumni, parents, town officials, and so on). This way people know that others see them as playing important roles in the endeavor.

Checklist for Modeling the Way

_____ Clarify your *personal credo*—the values or principles that you believe should guide your leadership behavior. Then talk about your credo with others in your organization (or team, club, class, community, program). Post this information prominently for everyone to see.

_____ Keep track of how you spend your time. Check to see whether your actions are consistent with what you and your colleagues have agreed is important. If you find inconsistencies, figure out what you need to do to align your actions with those values.

_____ Keep your daily planner at hand. Write down your promises as you make them. Review them daily and fulfill them on schedule.

_____ Develop a list of questions that you can ask at meetings to find out whether your team members are living out the team's values.

_____ Admit your mistakes. Say "I don't know." Show that you're willing to change your mind when someone comes up with a better idea.

_____ Set goals that are achievable. Tell people what the key milestones are so that you and they can easily see progress.

_____ Use analogies. Help others at the beginning get started by visualizing what their project will be like. It's sort of like planning a holiday: Think about how great it will be to get there, and start making plans for all the little things that will be required to make this happen. Then start taking action on those little things.

_____ Make it easy for others to say "yes." You don't need complete commitment at the beginning, just enough willingness to take some action in a general direction. Ask people to do what they are capable of doing, and then a little bit more.

_____ Make sure you wander around. Don't make people work to find you; go out and find them. Mingle. Just say "hi" and learn about what they are doing.

_____ Choose some people you consider to be role models. Learn whatever you can about them by reading biographies, watching films, interviewing, or spending some time with them.

_____ Visit a retail store that's widely acknowledged for its extraordinary customer service. Watch and listen to what store employees do and say. Interview a couple of the employees about how the store got such a stellar reputation. Apply these lessons to your own situation.

_____ Take a class in storytelling. Take a class in goal setting, on values clarification, on time management, or in active listening.

_____ Allow less experienced members to "shadow" you as you go about completing tasks and projects for your organization.

★ Checklist for Encouraging the Heart

_____ Wander around your "office location" for the express purpose of finding someone in the act of doing something that exemplifies the organization's standards. Find a way to recognize that person on the spot.

_____ Plan a festive celebration for each small milestone your team reaches. Don't wait until the whole project is finished to celebrate.

_____ Tell a public story about a person in your organization who went above and beyond the call of duty.

_____ Ask your teammates to help design a reward and recognition system for your organization (or group, club, project, community, chapter). Talk with others about how they would like to be recognized for their accomplishments or successes.

_____ Give people tools they can use to recognize one another, such as index cards or notepads printed with the message "You made my day" or "You are a hero." Create a culture in which peers recognize peers.

_____ Be creative about recognition and rewards. Try photographs, buttons, banners, ribbons, stuffed animals, painted rocks, special T-shirts, hats, and so on. Usually it's the thought, not the gift, that counts the most.

_____ Say "thank you" when you appreciate something that someone has done.

_____ Write at least three "thank you" notes each week.

_____ Create a "Hall of Fame" for your organization—an area (for example, bulletin board) in which to recognize all the people who've done extraordinary things.

_____ Attend an award ceremony for someone on your campus or in your community and make notes on what you like about it. Try some of the same methods the next time you hold an award ceremony.

_____ Ask for advice and coaching from someone you know who's much better than you are at recognition, saying "thank you," and celebrating.

_____ Take an improvisational theater class. Take a class on creativity, drawing, painting, or photography—to build your expressiveness skills.

_____ Ask people in your organization how and when they like to be recognized. Create a list with this information and distribute this throughout the organization.

_____ When you receive a "thank you" note about someone in your group, make it public by reading it out loud at a meeting, posting it on a bulletin board (with an additional note of appreciation from you), or publishing it in your newsletter or web page.

APPENDIX C

Normative Data for the *Student LPI*

Student LPI Scores for Greek Chapter Presidents (N = 177)

Challenging the Process	23.08
Inspiring a Shared Vision	24.07
Enabling Others to Act	25.58
Modeling the Way	23.66
Encouraging the Heart	25.54

Student LPI Scores for Resident Assistants (N = 333)

Challenging the Process	21.74
Inspiring a Shared Vision	20.66
Enabling Others to Act	25.20
Modeling the Way	23.25
Encouraging the Heart	22.23

Student LPI Scores for Peer Educators (N = 152)

Challenging the Process	22.34
Inspiring a Shared Vision	23.16
Enabling Others to Act	25.76
Modeling the Way	23.15
Encouraging the Heart	25.36

Student LPI Scores for Student Body Presidents (N = 35)

Challenging the Process	23.86
Inspiring a Shared Vision	24.34
Enabling Others to Act	25.43
Modeling the Way	23.63
Encouraging the Heart	24.57

Student LPI Scores for Orientation Advisers (N = 78)

Challenging the Process	23.04
Inspiring a Shared Vision	24.85
Enabling Others to Act	25.94
Modeling the Way	23.14
Encouraging the Heart	25.49

Student LPI Scores for High School Students (N = 151)

Challenging the Process	21.62
Inspiring a Shared Vision	21.89
Enabling Others to Act	24.72
Modeling the Way	22.01
Encouraging the Heart	24.18

Student LPI Scores by Gender

	Males (N = 378)	Females (N = 484)
Challenging the Process	21.65	22.63
Inspiring a Shared Vision	21.18	22.52
Enabling Others to Act	24.54	25.79
Modeling the Way	22.30	23.48
Encouraging the Heart	22.31	24.44

Student LPI Scores: Reliability Data

	Internal (N = 1255)	Test-Retest (N = 37)
Challenging the Process	.66	.94
Inspiring a Shared Vision	.79	.93
Enabling Others to Act	.70	.95
Modeling the Way	.68	.91
Encouraging the Heart	.80	.96

APPENDIX D

Computerized Scoring Software Instructions

The Student LPI Scoring Program is available from Kouzes Posner International (phone or fax 408–354–9170, or write to 15419 Banyan Lane, Monte Sereno, CA 95030). It costs $25.00, including first-class postage, and it is reusable (that is, it can be used again and again with different groups or classes). The software program can handle a group of up to eighty "self" respondents and nearly five hundred observers.

At the moment, however, only an MS-DOS based version of the scoring software is available. For those using Windows, it requires going to the Start icon, selecting Programs, then clicking on the MS-DOS prompt. From there the on-line documentation in the program takes one through the steps necessary for data entry and printing.

Following is a suggested design for using the computer-scored results in the workshop process. This design would replace the steps listed for "Scoring and Interpreting the *Student LPI*."

1. Having explained the leadership framework and assured the students that the *Student LPI* is a valid and useful instrument, you can distribute to students their copies of the *Student LPI* Feedback Report. Since there is a cover sheet for each person, students can assist in handing these out without compromising anyone's confidentiality.

2. Ask students to direct their attention to you for a few minutes while you explain how to interpret the data each person has been provided. Assure the students that they will have time for further study and reflection on their feedback.

3. Ask students to look at the summary page from their *Student LPI* Feedback. Example 1 on page 79 at the end of this appendix can be used as an overhead transparency. This page typically has the person's name ("profile for . . ."), current date, and school or class name at the top of the page. Below this information are a number of column headings.

4. Direct students' attention to the first column heading labeled "Self-Rating." This column indicates the student's assessment of his or her own behavior on each of the five leadership practices (Challenging, Inspiring, Enabling, Modeling, and Encouraging).

Explain that each of these scores can range from a low of 6 to a high of 30 because each practice is the summation of the responses to six statements, each statement using a five-point scale where a response of "1" indicates that this behavior is seldom or rarely used and a response of "5" indicates very frequent use of this behavior.

5. Ask students to look at their scores in this column. If you're using the example as an overhead, label this column "A." Ask participants to write "1" by the highest number in this column and to continue to rank the scores in this column from 1 for the highest score to 5 for the lowest score.

Ask students to consider that the practices they ranked 1 and 2 represent the practices (and behaviors) they feel *most comfortable* with or that feel most natural. Similarly, ask students to consider that the practices they ranked 4 and 5 represent those practices (and behaviors) that feel least comfortable or most awkward, that they underappreciate the importance of, or that represent missed opportunities for participation.

Note: Step 6 through Step 9 below require that students have feedback from other people (Student LPI-Observer scores). If only Student LPI-Self scores are available, these next four steps should be skipped. In any case, now, and again later, you will want to encourage students to collect more data, especially from other people, if they really want to know more about their impact as leaders.

6. Ask students to look at the columns for "LPI-Observer Ratings" and the first one marked AVG ("Average"). This column represents the average (mean) scores of all the people other than the student who completed the *Student LPI*. That is, if you simply added up the scores across the row marked "Challenging" under columns "A," "B," "C," "D," and so on, then divided by the number of people who completed the Student LPI-Observer, you would arrive at the average (mean) score. If you are using the example as an overhead, mark this column with the letter "B."

Ask students to look at their scores in this column. Ask them to place the number *1* by their highest number in this column and to continue to rank the scores in this column from 1 for the highest score to 5 for the lowest score. Now ask students to consider that the practices they ranked 1 and 2 represent those practices (and behaviors) that *other people* feel they engage in most frequently and with which they are *most comfortable* or natural.

Ask the students to consider that the practices they ranked 4 and 5 represent those practices (and behaviors) that *other people* feel they engage in least frequently and are *least comfortable* with, or that they feel most awkward with.

Or perhaps the student underappreciates the importance of that practice, or has missed opportunities for participation in that area.

7. Continue by asking students to look next at the relationship between the rank order of their Student LPI-Self ratings and their Student LPI-Observer ratings and to note the similarities between these two rank orderings. On the overhead transparency, you can write the letter "C" between your marks for columns "A" and "B" and ask students to think about the extent to which their self-perceptions are consistent with the perceptions of the people with whom they work and interact (as noted in the Student LPI-Observer scores).

Disregarding the absolute scores for a moment, this reflection focuses on the match (or mismatch) between self and other perceptions of "reality" (leadership). You can ask students, "Which of these two columns (A = Self or B = Observer) is the better representation of *reality*? If I didn't know you, but only had the *Student LPI* scores provided by you and provided by other people who interacted with you, whose scores would I consider the best representation of how you actually behave?" The response from students generally will be "the scores or assessments of others," and this is true.

That is why it is important to look at the degree of agreement between the two rank orderings. Even though there may be differences between the absolute scores from the Self and Observer columns (that is, "25" is not the same as "23.6"), it is possible that both parties will agree on the rank order of this practice, indicating agreement on the strength of this leadership behavior versus the others.

In the example provided for the group, the absolute scores do differ but the rank order is identical. You will want to point this out to the group, noting that while improvement is still desirable in the various practices, this sample student's own perceptions of strengths and areas for improvement are consistent with the views of others.

8. Next, direct the attention of the students to the column labeled "STD DEV," and explain that this is an abbreviation for "standard deviation." The standard deviation represents the extent to which Student LPI-Observer scores vary from the mean (average) score. A standard deviation of zero ("0") would mean that everyone gave exactly the same score or response to the statements. As the standard deviation increases from zero, so does the extent to which the responses provided by others vary from one another.

For the *Student LPI*, the standard deviation might be thought of as a measure of consistency (or inconsistency) in the way that other people view one's leadership behavior. The more everyone sees a person in the same way on these statements, the lower (closer to zero) the standard deviation. If each observer views that person quite differently on these behaviors, the standard deviation will be high. A quick way to look at this is to note that as the range between one's lowest and highest scores increases on any leadership practice or behavior (statement), the standard deviation also increases.

In the example, you can point out that the difference between the lowest and highest Student LPI-Observer scores on Inspiring is 6, which represents a standard deviation of 2.3, whereas the difference between high and low scores on Modeling is 10, which represents a larger standard deviation of 3.6.

For interpretation purposes, a standard deviation less than 2.0 is considered to be "low" and a standard deviation greater than 4.0 is considered to be "high." Standard deviations between 2.1 and 3.9 are referred to as "moderate."

All things equal, lower standard deviations are preferable to higher standard deviations because they imply a greater amount of agreement among other people in how they view the student leader behaving. However, higher standard deviations might be very understandable, and not problematic, to the student. That is, high standard deviations may be explained by the fact that the people who completed the Student LPI-Observer do indeed interact with the student leader in significantly different ways; it is not altogether surprising that they would have different views of his or her behavior (which is one reason that in the pre-session instructions we ask respondents to select people who have worked with them on a regular basis).

For example, high standard deviations would not necessarily be unwarranted if the Student LPI-Observer respondents were the student's manager, a close friend, a member new to the group, the departmental secretary, and the faculty adviser. The individual student must ultimately be the one who determines whether her or his standard deviation scores are problematic.

9. Point out the columns marked with the letters "A," "B," "C," "D," and so on; note that these represent the actual scores on the five practices from each person who completed the Student LPI-Observer. This allows students to see the overall assessment of their leadership practices by each individual Student LPI-Observer respondent. Students can note where there is agreement and disagreement among these respondents about their strengths and areas for improvement in these leadership practices.

This is a good point at which to explain to the students that the Student LPI-Observer respondents are not individually identified and that often people wish they knew exactly who these individuals were so that they could better understand the feedback. We suggest resisting the desire to figure out the identities of particular individuals; it is more important that students attempt to understand what this person or these people are trying to tell them. In any case, earlier research indicated that participants were only about 25 percent successful in matching names with scores.

Explain that the tradeoff is generally between identification (nonconfidentiality) of respondents and quality of data. Student LPI-Observer respondents are more likely to give better (more honest, more candid) responses—positive as well as negative—when they don't have to worry about being identified. We have opted for high-quality data; at the end of this session we will offer several strategies for collecting more data and finding out more from these particular people about their opinions of one's leadership effectiveness.

10. Ask students to look at the "Chart for Graphing Your Scores" (page 19 in their workbooks) and also to look at the summary sheet from their *Student LPI* Feedback printout. They should graph the scores from the "Self-Rating" column of their *Student LPI* Feedback on the chart and mark these points with the letter "S" (as described earlier, in step 10 of the "Scoring and Interpreting the *Student LPI*" section). Then they should connect these points with a *solid line* and label the end of this line "Self." You may draw this information on the overhead transparency yourself, so that they will understand more clearly what you are talking about, using the data from the sample *Student LPI* Feedback.

Note: Again, the next two steps (11 and 12) assume that Student LPI-Observer data has been collected.

11. Ask students to graph the scores from their Student LPI-Observer "Average Rating" column on the "Chart for Graphing Your Scores" and to mark these points with a letter "O". Then they should connect these points with a *dashed line* and label the end of this line "Observers." Do the same thing yourself; draw this information on the overhead transparency (Overhead 7), using the data from the sample *Student LPI* Feedback found in Example 1.

The "Chart for Graphing Your Scores" provides students with a visual picture of the match between their self-perceptions and the perceptions of others about their leadership practices.

- Attention should be directed to how parallel the two lines are— indicating relative agreement about both strengths and areas for improvement.
- Attention should be directed to practices where there are significant gaps between self and observer ratings—indicating areas for improvement.

12. On the "Chart for Graphing Your Scores," explain the column marked "Percentile." The percentiles represent the scores nationwide from students who have completed the *Student LPI* (over 1,200).[20] As scores are *normally distributed* (in the classic bell-shaped curve), most people's scores fall at the 50th percentile (roughly half of the scores fall above and roughly half of the scores fall below) and nearly two-thirds of all scores fall within one standard deviation of the mean.

Give students a few moments to look at the data on the "Chart for Graphing Your Scores" and compare themselves *normatively* with other students across the country. Although this is interesting (and often requested by students), it should be pointed out that this comparison doesn't necessarily say much about leadership for any particular person in any specific organization or organizational context.

Because leadership is a skill, you will want to observe that the important point for students is to determine what it will take for them to improve their base level of leadership ability, regardless of where they are relative to others.

20. The percentile scores represent only those from the Student LPI-Self.

Option: The *Student LPI* Scoring Program does compute average scores and standard deviations for both Student LPI-Self and Student LPI-Observer scores for *all* students in a workshop. It is sometimes more relevant (and interesting) for students to compare themselves with their peers in the workshop. If you desire, you can distribute this information to all students, or, when asking students to graph their own scores in steps 10 and 11, you can graph this particular group's scores (rather than the sample *Student LPI* Feedback scores) on the overhead transparency, then point out to the group whose scores these lines represent. Some interpretation of the group scores should be provided. If you are going to be offering multiple leadership development workshops, you may find it useful to accumulate the data from individual sessions and develop a campus *Student LPI* profile.

13. Direct students' attention to the next page of their *Student LPI* Feedback (see Example 2 at the end of this appendix). On this page are the thirty leadership behaviors arrayed from top (most frequent) to bottom (least frequent) according to the average responses to these statements from their observers.

Have students pay particular attention to at least the last five leadership practices. These are the ones that hold the greatest promise for improving the student's leadership effectiveness. Students should also be aware of their top five leadership practices and should be encouraged to continue practicing these behaviors.

Call students' attention to any asterisks in the far-right column. These indicate a difference greater than 1.0 between their self-perception and the perception of others. Students may want to think about how to reduce the gaps between these two perspectives.

14. Pause for a moment and make certain that everyone is ready to continue going over the *Student LPI* Feedback as one group. Remind them that in just a few moments you will stop talking and give them some quiet reflection time for further understanding the impact of their leadership feedback.

15. Ask the students to turn to the next page in their *Student LPI* Feedback (see Example 3 at the end of this appendix). They should note that this page is headed "Challenging the Process" and follows a similar format to the summary page. What this page reveals are the six statements (behaviors) that make up the Challenging the Process leadership practice (scale). Point out that the column headings are like those described previously and that they can be similarly interpreted. For example, on the first statement the sample person's own response was 3, while the average response from others was 2.6 and the standard deviation on this statement was 1.2.

16. Have students look especially at the specific responses to these statements and circle any of their own and/or others that are marked with either a

"1" or "2." Suggest that these behaviors especially represent opportunities for improvement.

17. Explain that there is a page like this one on Challenging the Process for each of the five practices, each organized in the same manner. Students should carefully work through these pages on their own, noting the leadership behaviors (statements) that they see as strengths and those they see as problematic or as areas for improving themselves as leaders.

To facilitate this individual assessment and interpretation, ask participants to look at pages 21–23 in their workbooks. These pages provide space for students to make sense of their feedback and to begin thinking about actions they can take to improve their leadership skills.

18. Point out that after working through the five separate leadership practices, they should consider again their overall leadership strengths and areas for improvement. Page 26 in their workbooks provides space for them to make summary comments on strengths and areas for improvement.

19. Now it's time for you (the facilitator) to stop talking. Let students know that this is their time to review their *Student LPI* Feedback individually, reflect on the data, and make notes to themselves in their workbooks in response to the questions asked. Provide students with sufficient time to accomplish this. This is also a time for students to ask you any specific questions they have about their feedback.

You now have several options on how to proceed, depending on the time available and your learning objectives.

20. You can either ask students to continue with their individual analyses through the Action-Planning Worksheet (Overhead 11) on pages 30–31 in their workbooks, or you can convene everyone at a particular time to focus their attention on this worksheet.

21. Start by offering students some ideas for moving from analysis to action. You may want to use the "Prescriptions for Meeting the Leadership Challenge" (Overhead 10), which are on page 27 in their workbooks. There are ten ideas, two for each leadership practice, that we have suggested as quick ways to get started. You can say a word or two about each prescription, providing an example or illustration.

We find it helpful to ask students to put a checkmark by each idea that they think they could do *right away*. Then we suggest that students select one or two of those that they checked and complete the Action-Planning Worksheet for how they will put these suggestions into practice in their organization (or club, group, team, community, project).

Also, in Appendix B there are expanded checklists of ideas for implementing each leadership practice, which you may want to use here or elsewhere in the workshop. The checklists can also be distributed as handouts or made into overhead transparencies.

Although students can use these ideas immediately, you might instead suggest that students use these ten ideas as a starting point for brainstorming other ideas that will make more sense for them in their circumstances.

22. Encourage students to select at least one leadership practice or behavior in which they can improve and to create an action plan for doing so.

Note: The Action-Planning Worksheet can be completed as a take-home assignment following the workshop or class. It can also be used as the basis for a follow-up leadership development program.

Example 1: Summary Page

```
            LEADERSHIP PRACTICES INVENTORY
                   STUDENT VERSION

              Profile for L. D. Ship

          Leadership Seminar Such and Such
              University or College XYZ
                    Today's Date
```

	SELF-RATING	LPI-OBSERVER RATINGS						
		AVG	STD DEV	A	B	C	D	E
CHALLENGING THE PROCESS	20	21.0	3.0	22	25	22	20	16
INSPIRING A SHARED VISION	21	22.2	2.3	20	25	24	23	19
ENABLING OTHERS TO ACT	26	24.2	3.1	22	28	25	26	20
MODELING THE WAY	24	22.6	3.6	20	25	27	24	17
ENCOURAGING THE HEART	25	23.6	3.3	26	22	25	27	18

Example 2: Leadership Behaviors Ranked

```
                    LEADERSHIP PRACTICES INVENTORY
                           STUDENT VERSION

                       Profile for L. D. Ship

                   Leadership Seminar Such and Such
                      University or College XYZ
                           Today's Date

              Leadership Behaviors Ranked by LPI-Observer Scores
```

			SELF	OBSERVERS	
VERY FREQUENTLY OR ALMOST ALWAYS 5					
8. Treats others with dignity and respect	ENABLING	5	4.6	
20. Gives appreciation and support to team	ENCOURAGING	5	4.6	
12. Communicates positive, hopeful outlook	INSPIRING	5	4.4	
18. Develops cooperative relationships	ENABLING	4	4.4	
24. Consistently practices espoused standards	MODELING	4	4.4	
15. Gives praise for a job well done	ENCOURAGING	5	4.2	
23. Creates atmosphere of mutual trust	ENABLING	5	4.2	
FAIRLY OFTEN 4					
3. Involves others in planning actions	ENABLING	5	4.0	
10. Recognizes people's contributions	ENCOURAGING	5	4.0	
27. Contagiously enthusiastic about future	INSPIRING	2	4.0	*
1. Seeks out opportunities to challenge skills	CHALLENGING	3	3.8	
14. Ensures agreed standards are adhered to	MODELING	3	3.8	
16. Looks for innovative ways to improve	CHALLENGING	4	3.8	
17. Enlists a common vision to realize interests	INSPIRING	3	3.8	
19. Shares own leadership beliefs and values	MODELING	3	3.8	
25. Finds ways to celebrate accomplishments	ENCOURAGING	3	3.8	
28. Provides opportunities for others to lead	ENABLING	3	3.8	
5. Encourages people along the way	ENCOURAGING	3	3.6	
9. Ensures work is broken into manageable pieces	MODELING	5	3.6	*
21. Asks "What can we learn?" from mistakes	CHALLENGING	3	3.6	
29. Ensures group sets clear goals and plans	MODELING	4	3.6	
2. Describes future possibilities for group	INSPIRING	4	3.4	
4. Explains own leadership style	MODELING	5	3.4	*
6. Keeps current on developments affecting group	CHALLENGING	3	3.4	
7. Shares aspirations about what could be done	INSPIRING	2	3.4	*
11. Challenges the way things are done	CHALLENGING	3	3.4	
13. Gives freedom to others to make own decisions	ENABLING	4	3.4	
30. Tells others about group's good work	ENCOURAGING	4	3.4	
22. Looks ahead and forecasts future	INSPIRING	5	3.2	*
SOMETIMES 3					
26. Experiments and takes risks	CHALLENGING	4	3.0	
ONCE IN A WHILE 2					
RARELY OR VERY SELDOM 1					

```
 *  Difference between Observers' and Self score was greater than 1.0
```

Example 3: Challenging the Process Page

```
               LEADERSHIP PRACTICES INVENTORY
                     STUDENT VERSION

               CHALLENGING THE PROCESS

                Profile for L. D. Ship

             Leadership Seminar Such and Such
                University or College XYZ
                     Today's Date
```

LEADERSHIP BEHAVIOR	SELF-RATING	LPI-OBSERVER RATINGS						
		AVG	STD DEV	A	B	C	D	E
1. Seeks out opportunities to challenge skills	3	3.8	0.7	4	5	4	3	3
6. Keeps current on developments affecting group	3	3.4	0.5	3	3	4	3	4
11. Challenges the way things are done	3	3.4	1.0	3	4	3	5	2
16. Looks for innovative ways to improve	4	3.8	0.7	4	5	4	3	3
21. Asks "What can we learn?" from mistakes	3	3.6	1.0	4	5	4	3	2
26. Experiments and takes risks	4	3.0	0.6	4	3	3	3	2
CUMULATIVE RATINGS	20	21.0	3.0	22	25	22	20	16

About the Authors

James M. Kouzes is chairman of TPG/Learning Systems, which makes leadership work through practical, performance-oriented learning programs. In 1993 *The Wall Street Journal* cited Jim as one of the twelve most requested "nonuniversity executive-education providers" to U.S. companies. His list of past and present clients includes AT&T, Boeing, Boy Scouts of America, Charles Schwab, Ciba-Geigy, Dell Computer, First Bank System, Honeywell, Johnson & Johnson, Levi Strauss & Co., Motorola, Pacific Bell, Stanford University, Xerox Corporation, and the YMCA.

Barry Z. Posner, Ph.D., is dean of the Leavey School of Business, Santa Clara University, and professor of organizational behavior. He has received several outstanding teaching and leadership awards, has published more than eighty research and practitioner-oriented articles, and currently is on the editorial review boards for *The Journal of Management Education, The Journal of Management Inquiry,* and *The Journal of Business Ethics.* Barry also serves on the board of directors for Public Allies and for The Center for Excellence in Non-Profits. His clients have ranged from retailers to firms in health care, high technology, financial services, manufacturing, and community service agencies.

Kouzes and Posner are coauthors of several best-selling and award-winning leadership books. *The Leadership Challenge: How to Keep Getting Extraordinary Things Done in Organizations* (2nd ed., 1995), with over 800,000 copies in print, has been reprinted into fifteen foreign languages, featured in three video programs, and received a Critic's Choice award from the nation's newspaper book review editors. *Credibility: How Leaders Gain and Lose It, Why People Demand It* (1993) was chosen by *Industry Week* as one of the five best management books of the year. Their latest book is *Encouraging the Heart: A Leader's Guide to Rewarding and Recognizing Others* (1998).